The Painter, the Cook and the Art of Cucina

The Painter, the Cook and the Art of Cucina

Anna Del Conte

Paintings by Val Archer

conran
OCTOPUS

This book is dedicated to L' Arte di Sacla' and the memory of Secondo Ercole and Piera Campanelle Ercole, who founded Sacla' all those years ago.

Published in 2007 by
Conran Octopus Limited, a part of Octopus Publishing Group
a Hachette Livre UK Company
2–4 Heron Quays, London E14 4JP
www.conran–octopus.co.uk

British Library Cataloguing-in-Publication Data. A catalogue record for this book is available from the British Library.

Publishing Director Lorraine Dickey
Managing Editor Sybella Marlow
Recipe Testing Mitzie Wilson

Design Caz Hildebrand and Julie Martin
Art Director Jonathan Christie

Production Manager Angela Young

ISBN: 978 1 84091 495 5
Printed in Italy

Contents

FOREWORD

The passion of my family to share and celebrate the art of Italian food has inspired the creation of this evocative book. The art of the painter and the art of the cook are similar in so many ways it is surprising that a book such as this has not been published before.

For me, my family and our colleagues, the enjoyment of delicious and tantalising Italian foods is also an art. At Sacla' we are known as 'those irresistibly Italian food people' because we are driven by a passion for the quality of Italian ingredients, the food cultures of our regions and by the intuition and preferences of cooks of all abilities who enjoy eating with their eyes as well as their palates.

It has been a great joy to work with Anna Del Conte and Val Archer, travelling through some of the relatively little known areas of Italy. Our experience has concluded that Italian cooking as such does not exist. The cooking of my country is really the cooking of its regions. Despite the fact that these regions are all very different, not least in what they farm and produce, cook and eat, the six in this book are starting to be discovered for the first time by visitors from overseas and are being enjoyed anew by Italians too. Most importantly, the people of these regions have a real love of food; its variety and seasonality, the regional specialties and recipes, the local producers, food customs and celebrations. There were many who generously shared their knowledge and hospitality on our journey, particularly local growers and many who work with Slow Food Presidia.

Anna Del Conte's knowledge of Italy, its people and its food, has made her one of the foremost experts on Italian cuisine and a great friend of our family. Anna's writings inspire us to visit little-known parts of Italy, whilst Val's paintings provide a warm and emotive visual feast of foods from the featured regions.

This is an inspiring and transforming book for anyone who loves the food of my country and the age-old Italian gift of making art out of life.

Cav. d. Lav. Lorenzo Ercole
President of Sacla', Asti, Piedmont

INTRODUCTION

This book is about the products, the produce and the cooking of just six regions of Italy – Piedmont, Veneto, Liguria, Le Marche, Puglia and Sardinia. It is not a cookery book: it is a gastronomic journey through the regions. We have chosen these six out of the twenty regions of Italy because they represent the cooking of the northern, central and southern parts of the peninsula very well, cooking that is extremely varied.

Piedmont offers a lot of outstanding produce, such as white truffles and peppers, products such as Castelmagno cheese and *gianduiotti*, and dishes – *salsa verde* and *bagna caûda* among others. It is a cuisine of northern Italy with French and Ligurian influences. I find the cooking of Piedmont one of the most exciting in Italy.

The cooking of Veneto is northern Italian too, but quite different, even if two of the Italian staples – rice and polenta – are favourites in both regions. The influence here is Slav, Austrian and Middle Eastern. On the whole it is less sophisticated than the Piedmontese, though by no means less interesting.

Liguria is still part of northern Italy and yet, because of its extremely mild climate, its produce and its products and cooking are definitely Mediterranean. Butter is not a cooking fat here, being totally replaced by the local sweet olive oil. Vegetable dishes are varied and interesting. Liguria is best known for producing basil as it is here that this plant grows best thanks to humid breezes from the sea and hot sun.

Le Marche, in central Italy, is still an untapped region that, because of its artistic and gastronomic treasures, deserves to be better known.

The same can be said of Puglia, the heel of the Italian boot. Puglia is the greatest producer of hard wheat and vegetables in the whole of Italy. The sea is rich in all kinds of Mediterranean specimens, from spiny lobster to sardines.

Of the two large Italian islands, Sicily and Sardinia, Sardinia is wilder and less well known. Its cooking, simple and traditional, is certainly worth exploring, as are the mysterious hinterland and the spectacular coast.

Each region has a chapter in the book, beginning with an introduction of its main characteristics and followed by seven or eight sections on various kinds of local produce and products, plus a description of a local *festa* – feast. The paintings are not confined to reproductions of what is in the text, although they are always close to it. They too, represent the most important elements, artistic and gastronomic, of each region.

In each chapter there are recipes that we have chosen because they are the most representative of the local cooking of that region. The recipes are not mine, except for a very few which I have adapted from recipes given to me by local people. The bulk of the recipes come from restaurants, directly from local cooks or from established authors. Most of the recipes can be reproduced in the UK but a few are based on a particular ingredient that is not available here.

This is a book that will enlarge the knowledge and appreciation of the regions, making it essential reading for any visitor, or anyone interested in the varied gastronomy of Italy.

Anna Del Conte

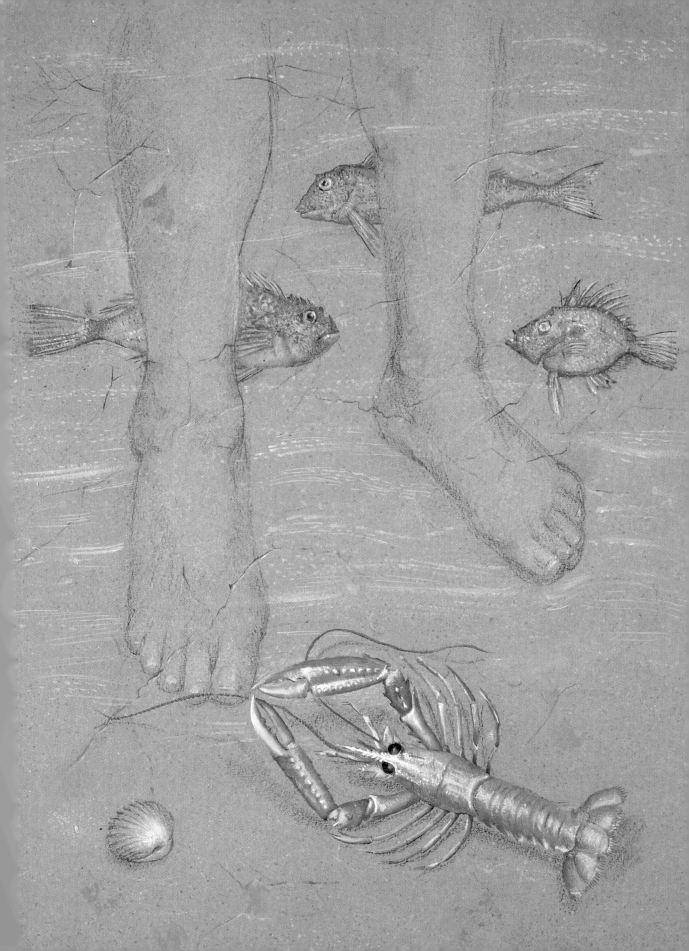

Piedmont

Last time I was in this region of
northern Italy I realized how apt its
name is – the foot of the mountain.
It was perfect autumn weather,
sunny and clear, with sharp nights
and warm days.

The countryside showed all the hues of red and yellow and green; the mountains were gunmetal grey against the mother-of-pearl sky at midday or the flaming sky of the sunset. They either looked like delicate Chinese paintings or like burning Turners. I drove around visiting the splendid castles of Venaria and Rivoli and the hunting lodge of Stupinigi, all built in the seventeenth and eighteenth centuries by the Savoia, the local monarchs who in 1862 became kings of Italy.

As usual my artistic pleasures were coupled with gastronomic ones. Of all regional foods, the Piedmontese is one of the most interesting and complex, both for its techniques and for its wealth of ingredients. Some of the dishes, such as the hare in civet, take two days to prepare; the meat *brasato* takes one day and the *bollito misto* is far more complicated than the boiled meat of any other region. On the other hand there is also a vast range of simple dishes, the origins of which are found in the rich vegetable gardens. Vegetables are often eaten raw, as in the famous *bagna caûda* (page 22). And it is no wonder, since some of the vegetables of Piedmont are indeed the best in Italy.

Suffice it to quote the asparagus of Santena, the squat white onions of Ivrea, the peppers and the turnips and the cardoons of the province of Asti.

Walnuts, chestnuts and hazelnuts from the Cuneo area are legendary, as are cherries, very important to the sweet-making industry. There is one variety, Bella di Garbagna, that is particularly suited to being preserved under alcohol because it keeps its texture and flavour well, or to being transformed into heavenly *boeri* (see page 51). And then there are the grapes with which some of the greatest wines in Italy are made.

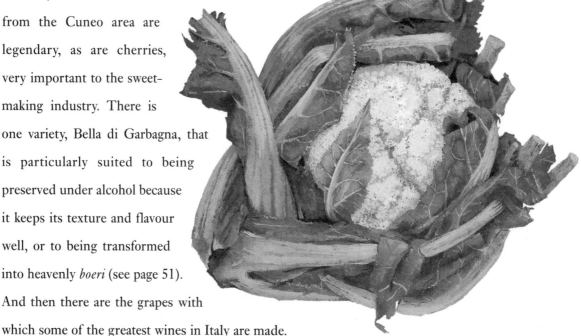

Piedmont not only offers some of the very best produce and products, it also boasts some of the greatest dishes. The list of *risotti* is long, and it must be headed by the elegant *risotto al tartufo*. At the other extreme of the social scale of *risotti* there is the *paniscia*, a rich peasant mix of rice, borlotti beans and other seasonal vegetables, plus a good glug of Barbera wine. Meat appears in most forms, ranging from raw in dishes similar to steak tartare or *carpaccio*, to cooked for several hours, as in the famous *brasati*, made with Barbera, Barolo or other great Piedmontese wines. Next to rice in most shapes and forms, the Piedmontese are particularly fond of polenta, which they often dress only with cheese, wild herbs or vegetables.

Nourishing peasant soups of tripe and trotters, bread and oxtail, rice and lamb offal are flavoured by *soffritti* of onion, garlic, sage and rosemary. Garlic figures more strongly here than in any of the other northern regions. So does olive oil, which in the old days came from neighbouring Liguria, together with preserved anchovies and salt. These came over the

Apennines along the Via del Sale, and the traders went back to Liguria loaded with maize, rice, hazelnuts, truffles, cheeses and other Piedmontese treasures.

But when speaking of Piedmontese food, one must not forget the cooking of the aristocracy, which was greatly influenced by the French. The union dates back to the first millennium when, thanks to the usual political marriage, Savoy and Piedmont became one and stayed one for over eight centuries. French was spoken by the aristocracy and French dishes were served at their tables, though they were French more in name than in flavour. The various soufflés, *fricandeaux*, *fricassées*, *civets* and *boudins* became *sformati*, *fricandò*, *fricassee*, *salmì* and *budini*. They were all italianized and the dishes, even at court, absorbed some of the earthy qualities of the *cucina povera*.

A legacy of the French influence is the richness of the *dolci al cucchiaio* – desserts – and of the rich buttery cakes that figure large on the Piedmontese table. *Zabaglione*, *panna cotta*, *bônet* (amaretti pudding), pears cooked in Barolo, *Monte Bianco*, *gianduja* cake, *coppa Torino* – a sort of *marron glacé* and crème patissière trifle – and stuffed peaches are certainly among the most delicious of Italian desserts.

The best-known Italian food, pasta, does not have a big role in the Piedmontese scenario. There are only two traditional pasta dishes there: *agnolotti* and *tajarin. Agnolotti* are ravioli stuffed with different sorts of chopped meats, usually braised, plus egg and cheese, and dressed with roast juices. *Tajarin* are very narrow tagliatelle; they can be dressed with a tomato sauce, with a chicken liver sauce, or, best of all, with butter and white truffles.

But before I close this far too short survey of Piedmontese food, let me tell you all I know about the best-known product of the region: *il grissino*, that thin, crunchy, delicate breadstick that mitigates so well the strength of the local cheeses, the porkiness of the *salumi* or the vivacity of an olive taken with vermouth or Campari, both Piedmontese creations, by the way. In Turin you'll find hand-made *grissini* in every bakery, so different from the industrially made ones, both in look and in flavour. The hand-made *grissini* are long, very long, irregular and softly friable.

Their origin is uncertain. A lovely story ascribes their invention to a doctor who, at the end of the seventeenth century, was looking after the delicate young Duke Vittorio Amedeo II of Savoy. He thought that the loaves of bread, called *gherse*, were too indigestible for the young prince and asked the local baker to make some very thin shapes, which were first called '*ghersini*'. However, there are doubts about the authenticity of this story, because in a travelogue of 1643 the author mentions having eaten 'bread as long as an arm and very very thin'. *Grissini* were a favourite of Napoleon, who called them *les petits batons de Turin*. Now they are a favourite of most people all over the world.

IL BOLLITO MISTO

One of the pleasures I look forward to when I go to Piedmont is dinner with Carlo Ercole in Asti. He and his lovely wife Lilli live in a beautiful house in what could be called Ercoleville, an expanse of green in the suburbs of Asti, where the four large houses of the various members of the family are set amid trees, lawns and shrubs. This is yet another pointer to the ties of the family in Italian life. Carlo is passionate about two things: art and food, which happen to be also my two greatest interests. With him conversation moves easily, from discussing the merits, and demerits, of balsamic vinegar for dressing salad, to the difference between a pot of Majolica of the Savona pottery and a dish from the Albissola pottery. My input, I must confess, is mainly gastronomic.

It is a real pleasure to sit at the Ercoles' table, where I have enjoyed some of the best food I have ever eaten. Superb Piedmontese dishes, with no distracting unnecessary embellishments, the emphasis being entirely on the great quality of the ingredients. I usually happen to be in Piedmont in the autumn. It is indeed the best time of year to eat the classic dishes of the region, and the time when some of the best local produce, such as the white truffle, is in season. It is the time when the grapes are harvested and the making of some of the greatest Italian wines begins.

During the many years I have eaten with the Ercoles I have had the festive *bagna caûda* with a rich assortment of local vegetables chosen by Carlo at the market in the morning, as well as splendid *agnolotti*, dressed with roast juices as they should be, rich *brasati* of Barbera di Asti, *risotti* with truffles and other outstanding dishes. Last year it was the turn of the *bollito con salsa verde*, which was preceded by a homely but perfect dish of *cardi gobbi gratinati* – gratin of cardoons – enriched by slivers of white truffle that Carlo grated over each serving with a generous hand.

The *bollito* was a hymn to the Fassone beef of the Razza Piemontese, a breed renowned all over Italy for the quality of its meat. The Fassone are animals of this local breed that have special attributes: they have very small bones, large breast and back and even larger hind thighs, with a small waist. When Aldo Strocco, a retired beef breeder and now the provider of excellent vegetables to the family hotel, the Ca'Vittoria, explained this to me, I concluded his description by saying, 'Like Sofia Loren.' '*Bravissima, proprio come Sofia Loren,*' agreed Aldo. These animals have a very tasty lean meat which is suitable for slow cooking, hence the great *bolliti* and *brasati* of Piedmont, and for eating raw in such dishes as the *carne all'Albese*, a sort of tartare steak in which the meat is always chopped by hand with a very heavy knife. Because of its lack of fat veins the meat is no good for grilling – it would simply char.

We went to see these animals at one of the farms of Sergio Giordano which is part of the Presidium of the Razza Piemontese beef. We were shown round the stables, full of cows in calf, and we admired the mums and babies just outside, while down in the distance we saw a group of these large white animals with funny short horns munching away in the field. Sergio told us how well fed these precious creatures are. They only eat natural food: maize, bran, broad beans and hay, which is better than fresh fodder because this would make the waist expand too much. They grow very slowly, as is natural, without any vitamin supplements.

The Fassone beef at the Ercoles' was certainly very good, tender and full of flavour. Carlo apologized for it not being a 'proper' *bollito*. There was only beef, no chicken, no calf's head, no *cotechino* and no tongue. 'But,' he continued, 'you can't make proper *bollito* for only five people,' as we were that night. *Bollito* is indeed a festive dish for at least eight to ten people, when it becomes *Il Gran Büi* – the great *bollito* (see page 20). I didn't mind; the beef was so good dipped into the most delicious *salsa verde*, a big bowl of it, with just a touch of garlic to enhance, but not overwhelm, the fresh parsley flavour. As a matter of fact in Lombardy traditional *salsa verde* does not contain garlic.

When I was a child, and herbs and vegetables were seasonal, the best parsley was said to be that which grows in southern Piedmont and in Brianza, north of Milan. These are indeed the two areas of Italy that compete with each other over the origin of *salsa verde*.

Carlo pointed out that there was no *cugnà*, and I was not altogether sorry. *Cugnà* is a mixture of wine must, quinces, sugar, walnuts and, sometimes, pears. It used to be eaten mainly with *bollito*, but now it is more often served with strong cheese to slightly mitigate the harshness. Frankly, I find *cugnà* an acquired taste that I have never managed properly to acquire. *Mea culpa*.

That delightful and delicious supper in November 2006 finished with another Ercole triumph, the *Monte Bianco di Lilli* (see page 53). It had just the right amount of chocolate and liqueur to modify the chestnut flavour, making it a touch less heavy and more interesting. It also looked splendid spooned into dessert plates from the pottery of Mondovì, which we had visited the previous day. Lilli told us that these plates were modern copies of traditional Mondovì patterns: a strong blue border with a primitive design in the middle. Lilli's plates had attractive bunches of flowers. The ultramarine blue border made a perfect surround to the dark brown of the chestnut purée and the pure white of the whipped cream.

Lilli made the pudding with raw chestnuts in the proper way, as indeed it should be done. When I told her about peeled chestnuts under vacuum she was not very interested. Once again the dedication and love of my compatriots for producing the best food, never mind the time and labour, was brought home to me during that dinner of utter simplicity, but total perfection.

Bollito Misto all' Astigiana

Mixed Boiled Meats Asti Style

Carlo Ercole makes the best bollito misto I have ever eaten. He serves it with excellent salsa verde and salsa rossa, two sauces which have been successfully reproduced in his factory.

SERVES 10–12

2 large onions

3 carrots

3 celery stalks

2 bay leaves

500g/1lb shoulder of veal

500g/1lb veal breast

½ calf's head, if available

½ fresh chicken

½ capon, if available

a veal tongue

a calf's tail

500g/1lb cotechino sausage

salt

Cut all the vegetables into large pieces. Put plenty of water into a large saucepan with a pinch of salt, add the vegetables and bay leaves and bring to the boil. Add the shoulder of veal and breast and cook for about 1½–2 hours or more. Cook the other meats separately in different suacepans following the same method.

To complete this Piedmontese meat dish it is essential to include some pork meat, such as cotechino sausage. Cook it separately in boiling water.

When all meats are cooked and tender, leave them in their stock until you are ready to serve them. The meats should be served warm so heat them up if necessary. Drain and slice the meats and serve on warmed plates. Sprinkle the meat with a pinch of coarse salt, a ladleful of the stock and a little olive oil. Serve with Salsa Rossa or Salsa Verde (see opposite).

Bagnet Russ

Salsa Rossa

SERVES 6

2 medium-size red onions, finely chopped
1 carrot, finely chopped
2 garlic cloves, finely chopped
7 medium-size ripe tomatoes, peeled,
    deseeded and finely chopped

2 tablespoons extra virgin olive oil
1 teaspoon sugar
½ red chilli pepper
1 tablespoon red wine vinegar
salt

Put the onion, carrot, garlic and tomatoes into a pan. Add the oil, sugar, chilli, vinegar and a little salt and cook on a low heat for 1 to 2 hours, stirring occasionally. Purée in a blender or other food processor, then transfer to a bowl and adjust the texture with little more olive oil if necessary.

Bagnet Vert

Salsa Verde

SERVES 6

110g/4oz parsley
200g/7oz pickled vegetables,
    pickled onions and pickled gherkins
2–3 slices day-old soft bread, soaked in
    vinegar and squeezed to remove the excess
50g/2oz premium anchovies

2–3 fresh tomatoes, peeled and deseeded
1 garlic clove
8–10 capers
yolk of 1 hardboiled egg
chilli powder, to taste
about 150ml/5fl oz extra virgin olive oil

On a wooden board, chop all the ingredients together very finely with a sharp knife. Do not use a food processor. Put the chopped ingredients into a bowl and add the oil, stirring until you have a smooth, not too thick sauce and adding more oil if necessary.

LA FIERA DELLA BAGNA CAUDA

It was a splendid autumn day. The air was crisp and clean and the sun was warm and lazy. Some 10,000 locals and three English people were all converging on Nizza Monferrato, a town in southern Piedmont, to celebrate the grape harvest with *bagna caûda* and *vino novello* – new wine. The three English people were Val, her husband Roger and me (under these circumstances I felt more English than Italian), sheepishly following our leaders, Lucia Ercole and Sara Sacco Botto weaving our way through stall after stall, all gaily festooned with jumpers and skirts, belts and bags, bras and knickers, tablecloths and pillowcases. Round the corner the scene changed and, happy in our territory, we surveyed salami and cheeses, hazelnuts and chestnuts, cardoons and peppers, discussing how much we could fit in our suitcases on the journey home.

Eventually, with a *salame* here, a cheese there and some nuts on the next stall, we arrived at our destination – the *enoteca* Signora in Rosso, where Tullio Mussa, the organizer of the *bagna caûda* feast, was waiting to meet us. We went into the eighteenth-century cellars, where all the tables were laid for the lunch. I grabbed the usual *grissino* or two, so perfect when one is hungry because they just slightly tame your hunger without killing your appetite, and we were immediately ushered into the kitchen, where the chef, very handsome with his nineteenth-century beard, was surveying three very large pots of *bagna caûda*. Inside each pot there was another pot, just a little smaller, full of that divine sauce that was very slowly cooking in a bain-marie. Maurizio, the chef, told me that *bagna caûda* must never reach 100°C, but should cook for about three hours at 80°C to 90°C.

In another room there were dishes and dishes laden with the vegetables, ready to be brought to the tables. We sat down, and three bottles of *vino novello* were immediately placed in front of us, plus the *ghersa* – the local bread, cut into slices, and the *grissini*. Soon the feast began, by which time a very long queue of people had formed, all waiting for a free table. I noticed that the first in the queue remained there for the hour and a half we sat down at lunch, watching our every mouthful with envy. When I looked at them I felt uneasy and wanted to hurry up, but then I picked up another piece of cardoon and forgot all about them.

The quality of the local vegetables is what makes the *bagna caûda* in the Monferrato area such a good dish. First and foremost is the *cardo gobbo* – the hunchback cardoon, the only cardoon that can be eaten raw. And this is thanks to the labour-intensive way that it is cultivated. The *cardi gobbi* are blanched under earth, not under tunnels, and that is what keeps their flavour so sweet and their stalks so tender.

The next day we met a grower, Carlo Vaccaneo, in his fields of cardoons. Unfortunately, two days before there had been a very hard frost during the night. Some of the cardoons, instead of standing beautifully upright, had caught a chill and were miserably lying down. But in one field the plants were still standing straight, all tied up in a bundles ready to be bent over – hence the 'hunchback' – and covered with earth. They stay under the earth for thirty or forty days. In another field the cardoons were ready to be harvested. All the outside leaves and stalks of each plant are discarded and only the tender heart, the edible part, is kept.

These hearts were what we ate at the Signora in Rosso, together with the local peppers of Asti, so descriptively called *quadrati d' Asti* (squares), the Jerusalem artichokes, the crisp white cabbage, the celery and fennel, plus potatoes, beetroots and turnips which were cooked and sliced. Together with the two large vegetable dishes, a pretty serving girl placed the *fujot* on the tables, one for each diner. The *fujot* is an earthenware pot containing a nightlight at the bottom, with a saucer on top full of *bagna caûda*. You pick up a piece or a slice of your chosen vegetable, immerse it in the sauce and pop it into your mouth. Heaven! At the end the girls come round with some eggs, and you break these into the remaining *bagna caûda* and stir them up with a fork to finish your meal with scrumptious scrambled eggs. Actually, none of us did so that day; we had all had enough, so got up and left – to the happy applause of the people in the queue.

Bagna caûda is a very convivial dish that is eaten in the country at the end of the grape harvest. All the workers, mostly men, sit around the tables, while the women place a very large *fujot* in the middle of the table for everybody to dip the vegetables into. And the lot is washed down with litres of Barbera Novello, or other local new wine, the perfect way to end many days of hard work.

OPPOSITE: *Cardi gobbi*

Frittata di Zucchine

Courgette Frittata

Frittata is the Italian answer to the Spanish tortilla. It can be made with cheese, all sorts of vegetables and even with pasta.

SERVES 4–6

a handful of fresh flat-leaf parsley
1 garlic clove
7–8 tablespoons extra virgin olive oil
2 medium or 3 small red onions,
  finely chopped

4 large courgettes, chopped
5 large eggs, beaten
salt

Roughly chop the parsley and garlic together on a board and set aside. Heat 4–5 tablespoons of the oil in a 30cm/12 inch non-stick frying pan and add the onions and courgettes. Cook until soft and golden, stirring frequently. Add the chopped parsley and garlic and season with salt. Stir thoroughly, then put into a bowl and leave to cool. Wash the pan.

When the vegetables are cool, add the eggs and mix well. Heat the remaining oil over a low heat in the non-stick frying pan and add the egg mixture, spreading it out over the base of the pan. Turn the heat down as low as possible and cook very slowly for 10–15 minutes. When the eggs have set and thickened and only the top surface is runny, place under a hot grill for 30 seconds to 1 minute until the top is set but not browned. Loosen with a spatula and slide onto a warmed plate and cut into wedges to serve. Delicious eaten warm or cold.

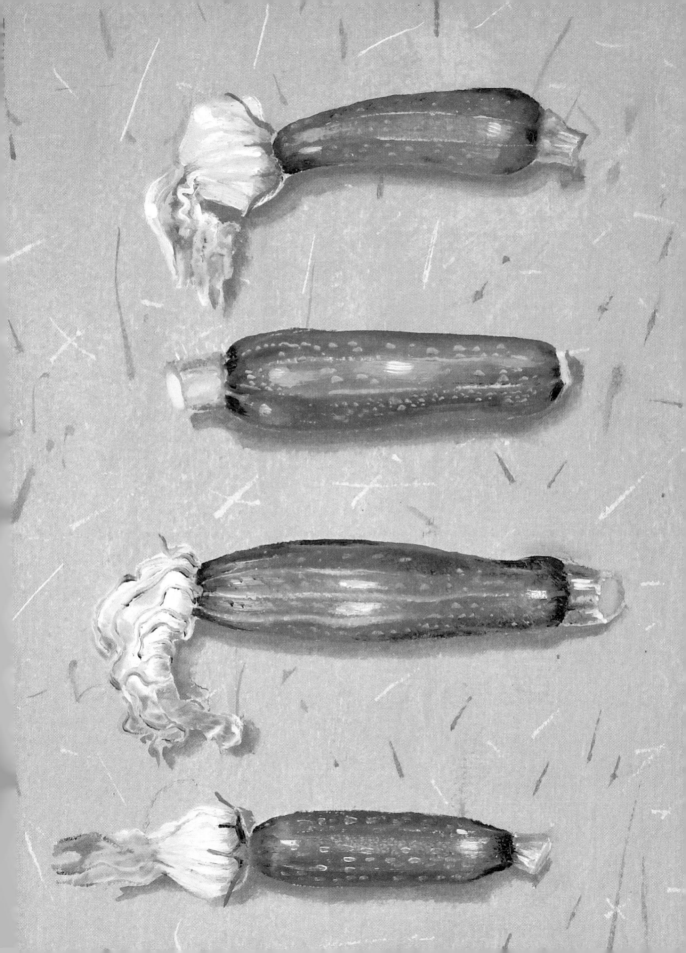

Peperonata

A classic dish from Asti where the best peppers are grown. The recipe is from the Ercole Family.

SERVES 8

1kg/2lbs red and yellow peppers
300g/10oz onions
400g/13oz tomatoes

100ml/3½fl oz extra virgin olive oil
2 tablespoons vinegar
salt

Wash the peppers, cut them in half and then remove the seeds and quarter them. Peel and chop the onions finely. Wash the tomatoes and quarter them, removing the seeds.

Gently fry the onions in a casserole with the extra virgin olive oil and add the tomatoes and peppers, sautéing them over a medium heat for 5 minutes. Simmer for 20 minutes.

Once cooked, (the peppers should not be too soft), add vinegar to taste with a good pinch of salt. Serve the Peperonata on a plate warm or cold. It is a perfect side dish for meats or polenta, but it is delicious on its own to eat with freshly baked bread.

LEFT: *A quadratto pepper*
OPPOSITE:
Corni di bue peppers

RICE

During one of my recent flights to Italy, my plane was stacked up before being able to land at Milan Linate. For some twenty minutes we were flying over and over an endless mirror, from which large farmsteads were sprouting here and there. It was an extraordinary sight. We were flying over the large area of the *risaie* – rice paddy-fields – in the provinces of Vercelli and Pavia, respectively in Piedmont and Lombardy. Looking down, I wondered if I could recognize the beautiful farmstead of the Principato di Lucedio, where a few years earlier I, with a few other journalists, had had an excellent lunch all based on rice grown on the estate. Different dishes were made with the many different varieties that are grown in the Principato. The Principato started as a Cistercian abbey in 1123 and in the fifteenth century the monks began to grow rice, this possibly being the first rice plantation in that area.

Rice was first cultivated near Naples, allegedly brought there by the Aragonesi. Another source claims that rice was brought to Italy by the Crusaders, and a third attributes the origins of rice in Italy to the merchants in Venice, who dealt with Middle Eastern spices and other goods from the East. What is sure is that by 1475 the cultivation of rice was sufficiently established in northern Italy for Gian Galeazzo Sforza, the Duke of Milan, to send a sack of seeds to the Duke of Este, assuring him that 'this one sack will give you 12 sacks of produce' – a ratio that, for the time, was indeed just short of a miracle.

And so rice became the popular crop of the wetlands of Piedmont and Lombardy. A very good species of rice, of the *japonica* variety, developed there, much better than any rice from other countries. As witness the fact that Thomas Jefferson, who loved Italy and anything Italian, from Palladio to pasta, decided to smuggle out a sack of seeds to plant in Monticello in Virginia. This was an illegal act, since the export of rice seeds was forbidden at the time.

Rice needs to grow in water, which, however, cannot be stagnant because the seedlings and young shoots

OPPOSITE: *Carnaroli rice with Mondavi crockery*

need a more or less constant warm temperature. The water is indeed called 'the thermal blanket'. Up to the 50s the cultivation of rice was very labour-intensive. The removal of the many weeds and the harvesting were all done by hand, mainly by women – *le mondine* – who were made famous by Giuseppe De Santis in his film *Riso Amaro* (*Bitter Rice*), one of the great neo-realistic Italian films of the post-war years. There was that unforgettable shot of Silvana Mangano, her skirt tucked up high, with water coming up to her knees, her low-cut jumper showing a very deep décolletage, bent double in the rice field. Some 3,000 people, mostly women, were employed in the fields. Now machines arrive and they do the work in one-twentieth of the time.

The seeds, planted in the spring, begin to develop panicles in about two months, making the rice field look like soft emerald green velvet. When harvest approaches in September to October, the plants begin to dry out and that cheerful green becomes a melancholy tawny. After the harvest the rice field is an even sadder sight, with little clumps of rotting straw. Milling is a skilled job, because good rice must have grains that are whole and perfect. In the showroom of the Principato di Lucedio there were little mounds of different varieties of rice, plus red rice and wild rice. These are new species that have only recently been brought on to the Italian market.

Italian rice is divided into four main groups: *ordinario*, *semifino*, *fino* and *superfino*. These groupings have nothing to do with quality, but only with the look of the rice, from small and round to long pointed grains. Each type of rice is used for different dishes; with *ordinario* Italians make soups and puddings, and so on, up to the *superfino* which is the ideal risotto rice. Having said that, the *semifino* Vialone Nano, with a smaller round grain, is also used in *risotti*, especially in Veneto, the region where it is mostly produced. Together with Carnaroli and Arborio, grown mainly in Piedmont and Lombardy, Vialone Nano is the most popular rice.

I like to use the right variety of rice for each particular dish. When I make a risotto from Veneto, such as *Risi e Bisi* (see page 89) or a risotto with mussels, I use Vialone Nano, while for a *Risotto alla Milanese* or a risotto with mushrooms I prefer a Carnaroli or an Arborio. These, however, are all *minutiae*. The important thing is that you use Italian rice for Italian dishes.

Risotto al Gorgonzola

Risotto with Gorgonzola

Two of the most popular produce of the region are united in this delicious risotto from the Hostaria I Due Ladroni in Novara.

SERVES 4

2 knobs of unsalted butter
½ onion, finely chopped
5 handfuls of Carnaroli rice
1 glass of white wine

1 litre/1½ pints meat stock
50g/2oz creamy Gorgonzola cheese
50g/2oz firm Gorgonzola cheese

Melt half the butter in a saucepan over a gentle heat, add the onion and cook until soft and golden. Add the rice, cook for a further minute or two, stirring, then add the wine. Cook for a few minutes more, to evaporate the alcohol, then start to add the stock a little at a time, stirring with a wooden spoon. The rice will take about 20 minutes to cook. After about 15 minutes, add the Gorgonzola. Before serving, stir in the remaining butter.

WHITE TRUFFLES

'The truffle is the diamond of cookery,' wrote Brillat-Savarin, while Alexandre Dumas put it even better: '... the ambrosia of the gods, the sacrum sanorum of gastronomes'. These two writers were certainly referring to the Périgord truffle, while Tobias Smollett, in his *Travels through France and Italy*, writes in 1766 that 'Piedmont affords white truffles, counted the most delicious in the world; they sell for about 3 livres the pound.' Oh, those were the days! This autumn, when I was in Piedmont, the price was 3,000 euros per kilogram and more for good specimens. Still, money is no barrier to those who want them.

The white truffle, the *tartufo di Alba*, or *Tuber Magnatum Pico* to give it its botanical name, grows mainly in Piedmont; and the best white truffle is the truffle found around Alba and Asti in southern Piedmont. It is found in woods, where it grows in symbiosis with poplars, willows, lime trees and oaks, between October and December.

Since Roman times agronomists have tried to cultivate truffles but '*Nascuntur et seri non possunt*' – they grow and cannot be cultivated, as Pliny the Elder said. They were very popular then, appearing on the emperors' tables. Nero called them *'cibus deorum'* – food of the gods – and so they were regarded all through the Renaissance.

The first-century AD book by Apicius contains six recipes for truffles. In most of them they are simmered with wine and herbs, which does not sound particularly good. But by the time of the Renaissance, truffles were often served raw, as they were at a banquet given by Cardinal Campeggi for the Holy Roman Emperor Charles V in 1536. The chef, Bartolomeo Scappi, in his book *Opera*, published in the middle of the sixteenth century, lists the whole menu and gives fascinating details of the table, relating that at the end of the dinner, when clean napkins were provided for the third time, small live birds were put into the napkins so that when the guests unfolded them, the room became full of fluttering, chirping birds. The truffles were served both cooked in a bitter orange sauce, and raw, just with salt and pepper. Giovanni Vialardi, the chef to Carlo Alberto and Vittorio Emanuele II, the first king of Italy, cooked the white truffles in butter, onion and Madeira, an odd recipe for a Piedmontese chef, unless one remembers how strongly the Savoy court was influenced by French cooking. This sounds very much like a French recipe for black truffles, which are always eaten cooked.

The Savoy kings were famous for organizing truffle-hunting parties and the European royal houses were keen to get experienced *trifolai* – truffle hunters – and trained dogs from the Savoy. In 1751 Carlo Emanuele III sent George II two *trifolai* and eight dogs to search for truffles in Windsor Park.

The great cookery writer Pellegrino Artusi, whose book *La Scienza in Cucina e l' Arte di Mangiar Bene*, first published in 1880, is still in print, gives us an odd recipe for white truffles. The very thinly sliced truffles are layered with equally thin flakes of Parmigiano Reggiano. Dressed with a good amount of olive oil, salt and pepper, they are brought to the boil and then the juice of one lemon is squeezed over them. But why cook them? And then he goes on and writes that *tartufi bianchi*, which he acknowledges are far superior to the black, are also eaten raw, dressed with lemon juice, salt and pepper.

And this is how my mother used to serve them at dinner parties in Milan. The truffles, gently rinsed and brushed at length with their special round brush (I often helped with this as a child) were sliced with the *'affetta-tartufi'* – the truffle mandolin – and piled over a third of a lovely glass bowl. The rest of the bowl was filled with sliced raw *Amanita caesarea*, the emperor of fungi, as its name implies, and flakes of Parmigiano Reggiano. Just lightly dressed with olive oil and a squeeze of lemon juice and salt and pepper, it was indeed a salad fit for an emperor.

I love truffles and loved them also as a child, when we ate them quite regularly during the autumn. They were far less expensive then than they are now, since more were found and far fewer people wanted them. There were none for me to eat when I came to London in the gastronomic desert of the 50s. Nobody had even heard of them. But slowly truffles appeared on the English scene and at the same time I became involved in writing about Italian cooking. This resulted in several most enjoyable hunts in Piedmont. I particularly remember one, when the photographer, two journalists and I flew to Asti for a hunt. The *trifolao* told me that it was a terrible year and he had found none so far. I simply said that he should bury a truffle, because the photographer had to take pictures of the dog digging. 'Fine,' he said. Next morning, a beautiful autumn day, at 7 a.m. we were away in the woods with Tita, a small unassuming mongrel on a lead. Off we went and off she went and after a well-staged hunt Tita 'discovered' the buried treasure, to everybody's relief. A few minutes later Tita is digging again in another spot and her master knows what she is after. He unearths a lovely example amid everyone's joy and jubilation. Tita was duly rewarded with two biscuits and a lot of '*Brava, brava*,' not such a big reward for two treasures. But she was happy, running around barking and wagging her tail.

These dogs may not be the most beautiful canine specimens, but their aptitude is uncanny. Only once did I come across a lovely-looking truffle dog – Diana – a smallish but beautiful sort of pointer. She won the first prize at the competition for the best truffle dog at the fair in Moncalvo. But Diana had stage fright and didn't want to go on to the podium to receive her medal, and she kept hiding between her master's legs. Apparently over the years she had always found the best and biggest truffles, and big is indeed beautiful in a truffle, just as it is in a diamond. Truffles are usually found just a few centimetres below the surface. The dog begins to dig with his front legs and then the *trifolao* comes with a small trowel and continues the digging, otherwise the dog would damage the truffle.

There is a closed season for collecting truffles, which starts on a variable date in October and ends at Christmas. White truffles have a very short 'sell-by' date but they can be preserved by sterilization, although they lose flavour. Or they can be pounded into a paste with other ingredients or infused in olive oil.

Preserved anchovies have been used in the cooking of that area for centuries. They were brought over the mountains, with the olive oil, from the Ligurian coast along the salt road since Roman times in exchange for Piedmontese goods. As a result, anchovies are the intrinsic flavouring of *bagna caûda*, the most ancient Astigiano dish. But the anchovies often used in combination with the white truffles are not from Liguria, because nowadays the catch of anchovies in the Mediterranean is not good. They come from the Bay of Biscay, where they have always been caught with the same centuries-old fishing method. They are preserved under salt for about three months. A fat anchovy pushed into a jar with a nugget of white truffle is a marriage made in heaven.

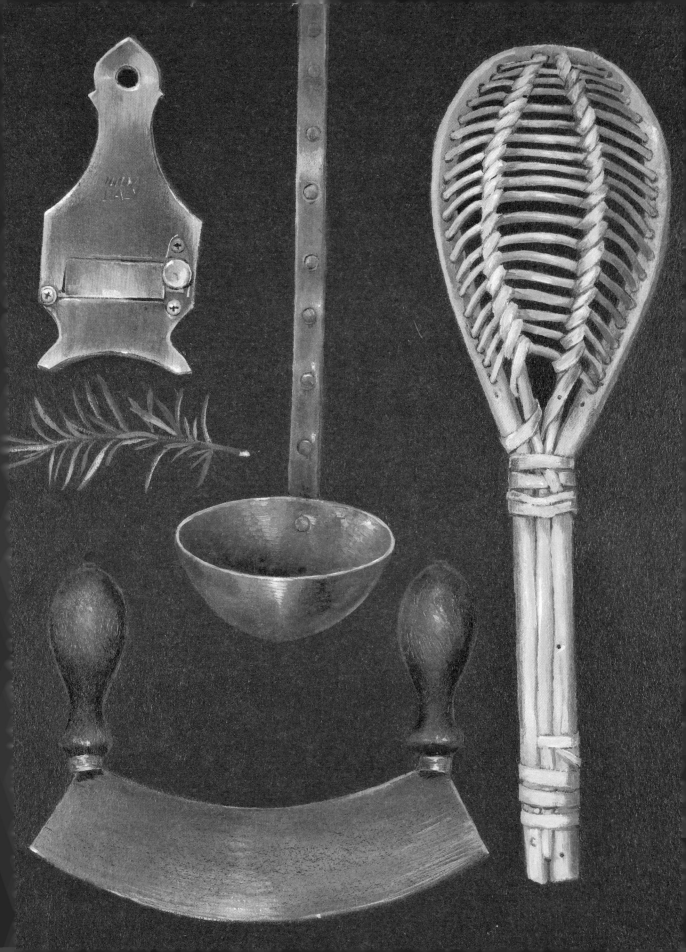

Carne Cruda con il Tartufo

Truffled Veal

This is the ultimate steak tartare made with the excellent local beef, the Fassone. This recipe comes from the Ristorante Ca' Vittoria in Tigliole, where Sandra and her mother excel in cooking local dishes.

SERVES 4

400g/14oz leg of veal
1 garlic clove (optional)
3 tablespoons extra virgin olive oil

salt and freshly ground black pepper
juice of 1 lemon
white truffle, to serve

Carefully remove any fat from the veal and cut the meat into pieces or slices. Put the meat on a wooden board and chop it very finely with a heavy, sharp knife until it looks like mince. Roughly crush the garlic, if using, and squash it up with a fork.

Put the meat into a bowl and add the garlic, oil, salt and pepper. Mix well, then let it rest for about 1 hour. Just before serving, stir in the lemon juice. Put the veal on a plate, shape it with a fork and top it with shavings of white truffle.

Golden rules

- The meat must be finely chopped with a knife, not in a mincer or a mixer.
- The garlic must be crushed and not cut.
- Lemon juice must be added at the very end to avoid 'burning'/'cooking' of the meat, which would make it grey and unappealing.
- Top with truffle when serving. If truffles are not in season, accompany the *carna cruda* with finely sliced *porcini* or other fresh mushrooms. Alternatively serve with a julienne salad of celery, turnips, endive and slivers of Parmesan, lightly seasoned with oil and salt.

Brasato Estivo a Tutti gli Ortaggi

Braised Veal with Vegetables

I have a book, *La Cucina del Piemonte,* written by one of the greatest gastronomic writers of my generation, Giovanni Goria. He was not a chef, but he had a deep knowledge of the traditional cooking of his region and he knew how to cook well. His recipes are sometimes sketchy, because he rightly assumes that anybody who likes to cook has a good basic knowledge. But, of course, he wrote in Italian and for Italian cooks. So I filled in what was missing, and the result was perfect.

SERVES 6

1 x 1.25kg/2lb 12oz veal joint, tied
salt and freshly ground black pepper
4 tablespoons olive oil
6 garlic cloves, peeled
2 sprigs of fresh rosemary
2 onions, thickly sliced

3 carrots, cut in chunks
1 large head of celery, thickly sliced
2 medium courgettes, cut in chunks
1 large red pepper, grilled, peeled and sliced
500ml/18fl oz meat stock

Preheat the oven to 150°C/300°F/Gas Mark 2. Season the meat with salt and pepper and brown it all over in a casserole or ovenproof dish in the hot oil with the garlic and rosemary. Lift the meat out of the casserole and set aside, discarding the garlic and rosemary. Put all the vegetables into the dish, lay the meat on top and pour over the stock. Cover loosely with foil, place in the oven and cook for about 2 hours, turning the joint two or three times.

When the veal is tender, take it out of the dish and place it on a board. Purée the cooking vegetables and check the seasoning. Carve the meat and serve with the vegetable sauce.

Brasato al Dolcetto

Braised Beef with Dolcetto Wine from Dogliani

Brasato is in northern Italy what roast beef is in Great Britain – a festive convivial dish which can be made with different local wines. This recipe, made with Dolcetto, was given to me by Pina Fassi, the chef-patronne of the famous restaurant Gener Neuve in Asti.

SERVES 6–8

2 tablespoons olive oil
1kg/2lb 4oz braising beef, in one piece
1 onion, sliced
½ carrot, sliced
2 celery sticks, sliced
2 garlic cloves, left whole

1 sprig of fresh rosemary
a pinch of cinnamon
salt and freshly ground black pepper
½ litre Dolcetto or other fruity
*   Italian red wine*
½ litre beef stock

Heat the oil in a casserole and add the beef, onion, carrot, celery, garlic and rosemary. Season with the cinnamon, salt and pepper, and cook for about 10 minutes, turning the beef to brown it. Add the wine and stock, bring to the boil then lower the heat and leave to simmer for 1 hour.

Remove the meat from the casserole and keep warm. Remove the rosemary sprig and bring the sauce to the boil and reduce by half. Purée the sauce with a hand blender until smooth. Slice the beef, pour over the sauce and serve with mashed potato or polenta.

FAMILY AND FRIENDS

It is in the kitchens of their homes in Asti that three generations of the Ercole family have learnt their love of food and it's importance in their lives, a philosophy they have extended to Sacla', the successful Italian company that they run so passionately.

As with most Italians, they are proud of their local foods, so their favourite meals always revolve around what is in season or in peak condition.

The cooking in most Italian homes is as good as in many restaurants, and the main meal of the day is invariably enjoyed at lunchtime, when almost everywhere seems to shut down for a few of hours to allow food, conversation and the occasion to be shared and savoured.

Italian people have a wealth of food knowledge and expertise. Even those who live in the towns have a thoroughly good knowledge of agriculture and the importance of food provenance and sustainability. They appreciate the freshness and quality of their raw ingredients and continue to place great emphasis on the family meal, traditional recipes and cooking skills. These values are not learnt through formal education but from families cooking and eating together and making time to enjoy the pleasures of the kitchen and the table.

So are there any lessons to be learnt from the Italian approach to food? Perhaps Carlo's son, Giuseppe, hits the nail on the head when he told me that 'the family who eat together stay together'.

'The pleasure of sharing food is the essence of family life for most Italians, and helps bring the generations together in the most convivial way.'
Carlo Ercole

THE CHEESES OF PIEDMONT

The northern regions of Piedmont and Lombardy offer the greatest selection of outstanding cheeses in the whole of Italy, a country that can boast a very large number of excellent cheeses. These include many cows' cheeses, a few ewes' and a few goats' cheeses.

Let me start with the one that unites these two regions: Gorgonzola, one of the most famous Italian cheeses. It had its birth in Lombardy, but is now made mostly in Piedmont. Gorgonzola was a village surrounded by luscious green pastures on the outskirts of Milan (it is now part of the asphalt jungle), and it is there that the cheese was created from the milk of cows that came down from the mountains to winter on the plain. Its origin is attributed to an innkeeper in Gorgonzola who used to be paid in cheeses by the shepherds who lodged at his inn. These cheeses were the soft, mild *crescenza*. One day a few of these developed greeny, mouldy streaks. Some customers tasted the mouldy cheese and declared it excellent. Gorgonzola was born. Nowadays the mould is added to the milk and the cheeses are then aged for two to three months in special storerooms. There are two kinds of Gorgonzola: *piccante* and *cremoso*, which has latterly become the more popular. All Gorgonzola must carry the stamp of its origin (DOP), which is applied by the Gorgonzola Consortium in Novara, eastern Piedmont.

A traditional and totally Piedmontese 'blue' cheese is the Castelmagno. It is made in the province of Cuneo with cows' milk and a small quantity of ewes' milk and aged for two to five months, when it develops bluish-green streaks all over and becomes strong and quite piquant. Castelmagno is judged by some cheese connoisseurs to be the greatest Italian cheese. Another cheese of mixed cows' and ewes' milk is the Montebore. It is claimed to have been the only cheese served at the grand Renaissance banquet at the wedding of Isabella d'Aragona, daughter of the king of Naples, to Gian Galeazzo Sforza, son of the Duke of Milan, in 1489. Montebore is produced in the south-eastern corner of Piedmont and its production has recently been revived by the Slow Food Foundation. It is a wonderful cheese, with a peculiar scent of sheep and spices, a fabulous buttery texture and a flavour that develops into an interesting grassy aftertaste. Depending on its ageing – from one week to two months – it is milky when fresh, cheesy when

OPPOSITE: *Robiola di Roccaverano*

semi-aged and when old it becomes a strong cheese mainly used for grating. There is a peculiar aspect of this ancient cheese which I must mention – its shape. Every Montebore consists of three round cheeses, one on top of the other, the largest at the bottom, the smallest at the top, like a wedding cake. Was it created like that on purpose for that famous wedding?

My favourite Piedmontese cheese is the Robiola di Roccaverano. There are quite a few *robiole* made in Piedmont and Lombardy, usually made from cows' milk or a mixture with ewes' and goats'. The Robiola di Roccaverano is a *robiola* that has been made for centuries with the milk of the Roccaverano goat. There is now a Presidium to protect the production of this cheese, the only *chèvre* that can compete with the French ones. We went to see the storerooms where the *robiole* made in small neighbouring dairies are salted and aged. When eaten after two or three days the cheese has a complex flavour of different herbs mixed with a tinge of goatiness, which becomes more pungent with ageing up to twenty days. I loved the fresh one, which has a minimal touch of goat in its pure white soft paste. A real delight.

When I was a child in Milan (and that was before the war), a woman used to come to our flat in the centre of the city. She was always dressed in black and she carried a large flat basket on one arm, with scales for weighing on the other. In the basket she had bundles of cheeses wrapped in muslin, all fresh white cheeses that I loved. My mother used to buy ricotta, mascarpone and *crescenza*. The ricotta was the Piedmontese one called Saras, fresh and richly milky, made with the whey of cows' milk, not ewes' like the better-known *ricotta romana*. They were little white shapes wrapped in hay. I rediscovered the delicate yet positive flavour of that ricotta after many, many years when, on my recent trip in Piedmont, I tasted it at breakfast at the hotel Ca' Vittoria, a charming hotel in the country near Asti where everything you eat is the best you have eaten. It nearly brought tears to my eyes, and it certainly brought a smile to my palate. There is now a Presidium to protect the producers of this ricotta, made in a few dairies in the lower Alps of Piedmont and Valle d'Aosta. Milk, and even cream, is usually added to the whey to produce a more tasty and richer ricotta.

I must also mention the *tome* and *tomini* – smaller edition. There are many different sorts of these cheeses – as many, so it is said, as the Piedmontese valleys. They are made with cows', ewes' or goats' milk or a mixture of these. They can be fresh, with a milky fresh flavour, semi-aged when they become piquant, or aged when they are quite strong. The *tome* favoured by the cognoscenti are those of the Langhe, the mountain chain in the province of Cuneo, a Piedmontese province from where a lot of the very best produce and products come. These *tome* are all made with ewes' milk, to which a smaller quantity of cows' milk is sometimes added. An interesting variation is made by preserving crumbled aged *tome* in earthenware pots with a glass or two of *grappa*, which makes the cheese more creamy and very strong. This concoction is called *bruss*, and it is one of the very rare foods that having tried once, I will not be trying again.

OPPOSITE: *Montebore 'wedding cake cheese'*

Gnocchetti di Ricotta con Funghi Porcini

Gnocchetti of Ricotta with Porcini Mushrooms

Another recipe from the restaurant Ca' Vittoria, a delicious and welcome change from the more common *gnocchi di patate*.

SERVES 4

500g/1lb fresh ricotta, drained
100g/3½oz Parmesan cheese,
   freshly grated plus extra to serve
3 egg yolks
2 boiled floury potatoes, drained
   and mashed
110g/4oz wheat flour

salt
3 tablespoons extra virgin olive oil
50g/2oz unsalted butter
400g/13oz porcini mushrooms, sliced
2 garlic cloves, chopped
1 tablespoon chopped flat-leaf parsley
white truffle to serve (optional)

Put the ricotta into a large bowl and add the Parmesan, egg yolks, potatoes, flour and a pinch of salt. Mix well until you have a dough that is soft and smooth but still firm enough to be worked by hand. Sprinkle a working surface with flour. Break off small amounts of dough and make them into rolls like breadsticks, then cut into small pieces about 1cm x 1cm to make the *gnocchetti*. Keep your hands well floured when shaping the *gnocchetti*.

Bring plenty of salted water to the boil in a large pan and cook the *gnocchetti* for 2–3 minutes, a few at a time to prevent them sticking together. Lift them out of the water as they come to the surface.

Heat the oil and butter in a pan. Add the mushrooms, garlic and a sprinkling of chopped parsley and cook gently, adding more oil if necessary. Put the mushrooms on a serving plate, add the *gnocchetti* and top with extra Parmesan and finely shaved white truffle if you have some.

TURIN AND ITS CAFÉS

Turin had a face-lift courtesy of the Winter Olympic Games of 2006, and is again the elegant beautiful city it used to be in its nineteenth-century heyday when it was capital of the Kingdom of Piedmont and Savoy. It has also managed to appeal to the young, who now stroll and lark about under the lofty arcades of Piazza San Carlo, mingling with sedate bourgeois middle-aged couples and families pushing buggies and flying balloons.

Up until the last war, Turin had been in the driving seat in quite a few fields, first and foremost the car industry, with the foundation of the Fiat factory in 1899 by Giovanni Agnelli. Fashion also had its birth in Turin in the 30s before surrendering its premiership to Florence after the war. Radio – the RAI – was first set up in Turin before moving to Rome, and so was television. But it is the cinema that glamorized Turin in the early days. The first silent films were made there and, as a tribute to those golden years, in 2000 the most important cinema museum was opened, thanks to the vision and perseverance of Maria Adriana Prolo, who during and after the war gathered enough enthusiasm – and money – to open this exhilarating museum in the Mole Antonelliana.

The Mole was built in 1889 by the architect Francesco Antonelli as a synagogue, but was never used as such. It is the tallest brick building in Europe – 168 metres – a sight that dominates Turin and has become its symbol. The museum, by the architect François Confino, follows the spiral ascent of the tower. It attracts throngs of young people, who in the evening move from one bar to the next for their 'happy hour', a custom that has conquered Italy. The young walk about, munching a *pizzetta* here, a *panino* there, a *tramezzino* in between, and holding a can of whatever drink they fancy, to the sound of live music being played at every corner.

Rather than a 'happy hour' crawl, Val and I chose to go on a café crawl. We started with the *caffè storico* Baratti & Milano, founded in 1858, where we had our elevenses. The Baratti & Milano has recently been renovated, and it is now showing the full splendour of its stucco, its furnishings and its wooden carvings. The Caffè Mulassano was our second port of call, a small café that opened at the beginning of the twentieth century and immediately appealed to the producers and directors of films, television and radio. The room is decorated with exquisite local marbles and the centre of the ceiling is in Madeira leather. It was at this café that the first *tramezzino* – small sandwich – was served in 1925, and is still a speciality.

We sat outside and had a hot chocolate, accompanied by *baci di dama*, almond biscuits with the lovely name of 'ladies' kisses', and *brutti ma buoni* (ugly but good), biscuits made with hazelnuts, both Turinese specialities.

Up we got and walked in beautiful sunshine, to the tempo set by a band of young Sicilians playing popular tunes on the blue and white bandstand, to the Al Bicerin, opposite the Chiesa della Consolata, the most beautiful and poignant baroque church ever. *Bicerin* means small glass, and it was in that exquisite small café, all wood *boiserie* and mirrors, that the drink that is now synonymous with Turin was created. It consists of a hot mixture of coffee, chocolate and cream, served – as its name implies – in a small punch glass. This, and hot chocolate, were the fashionable drinks of the nineteenth century and at this café they are both still made from the original recipes. It used to be the meeting place of the Turinese *intelligentsia* from Cavour to Calvino, who were joined by passing visitors like Nietzsche, Dumas and Puccini.

In all these places we were agog at the sight of all the different chocolates, *petites patisseries*, candied fruits, *marrons glacés* and countless other treats. Trays and trays of them, shiny and inviting, ready to be picked up and eaten, and jars and jars of *caramelle* (sweeties) in all shapes, sizes and colours of every description – all the sweet things for which Turin is so proudly famous.

In the evening we went to the Caffé Torino in the Piazza San Carlo for our aperitif, as James Stewart, Ava Gardner and Brigitte Bardot used to do in their heyday. Val had a Cinzano and I had a Punt e Mes, sitting on the high stools at the long curved bar in that beautiful room, full of golden mirrors and crystal chandeliers. We had our second aperitif just

a bit further along, at the Caffé San Carlo. This, one of the oldest cafés, having opened in 1820, boasts a big Murano chandelier that totally dominates the room.

At aperitif time all the cafés and bars in Turin are packed. The custom of the drink before the meal is two centuries old in that city, when Cinzano, Carpano and vermouth were invented. The first vermouth was in fact created by Giovanni Carpano. The Savoia loved it and used to send precious little bottles of it to the VIPs of the time. A 'Bottega del Vermut' was opened in Piazza Castello, and it is there that the first Punt e Mes was christened as such around the end of the nineteenth century. The vermouth was usually 'corrected' by a half quantity of bitter. One of the businessmen who were always crowding the café simply asked the barman for 'un punt e mes', meaning a glass of vermouth and a half of the bitters. Soon after, Punt e Mes began to be asked for by a silent gesture: one hand with thumb up in the air while the other hand was held horizontally next to it.

Neither Val nor I dared to ask for our drink like that. It was brought to us at our small marble table with little bowls of plain olives, neither stoned nor dressed, delicious salted almonds, tiny bread rolls covered with savoury gourmandises and flavoured *grissini*. We elegantly sampled only a few, keeping our appetite in good shape for our final tour-de-force at the Ristorante del Cambio.

There are very few cities in the world that have managed to keep a restaurant going so successfully for so long. The restaurant was opened in 1757. 'Today we made history and now let's go and eat,' said Camillo Benso di Cavour after declaring war on Austria in 1859, the war that led to Austria withdrawing from Italy and the subsequent creation of its kingdom. Cavour was a gourmet and the Ristorante del Cambio was his choice. Two and a half centuries later we sat opposite Cavour's table and had the same dishes, served on the same plates by waiters in the same uniforms – tails and black ties – surrounded by the same baroque-looking glasses, stucco, chandeliers, chairs and tables in their starched white damask cloths.

We ordered dishes that Cavour would have ordered. First and foremost *la finanziera*, that exquisite *intingolo – ragoût –* made with all the inside bits, plus the cockscombs, of a chicken, which I followed with a proper *vitello tonnato all' antica*, i.e. made without mayonnaise as in the traditional old recipe, and Val with a *brasato della vena al Barolo, vena* being a cut of beef of the Razza Piemontese breed – a sumptuous dish indeed. All the dishes were served without any fussy and superfluous decoration. We went back to the hotel happy and delighted with our day, regretting only our cowardice in the face of ordering a *zabaglione* or a *panna cotta* to close in glory our gourmand extravaganza.

GIANDUIOTTI, MARRONS GLACÉS AND ALL THINGS SWEET

When I think of chocolate, I dream of *gianduiotti*, those divine chocolates, suitably wrapped in gold paper, that when you bite into them release a soft ambrosian taste of chocolate mellowed by a nutty flavour. *Gianduiotti* are made with *pasta gianduia*, a mixture of bitter chocolate and chopped hazelnuts from Le Langhe. The creation of this paste is attributed to Michele Prochet, who decided to mix in some hazelnuts to offset the cost of chocolate, which had risen to stratospheric heights due to the continental bloc against Napoleon. As so often, every cloud has a silver lining. The odd name of these chocolates refers to their shape, which looks like the hat of Gianduia, the Piedmontese character in the Commedia dell'Arte.

Some years ago I went to the workshop of Guido Gobino, one of the greatest Turinese *chocolatiers*. It was an irresistible experience, even for me, a very selective chocolate eater. I found it extremely hard to keep my hands under control: one of them kept darting out to the nearest dark blob and then quickly into my mouth. Guido, second-generation *chocolatier*, has created a small edition of the *gianduiotti*, called Tourinot, which I like very much because of their size.

But Gobino is not the only outstanding *chocolatier* in Turin. There are quite a number of others, probably because it was in that city that the first solid chocolate was made,

thanks to a new machine invented by a certain Douret, or Doret, at the end of the eighteenth century. Douret became authorized *chocolatier* to Louis XVI, who granted the title of 'Chocolaterie Royale' to his factory. The Douret machine was extremely primitive, and at the beginning of the nineteenth century Caffarel started proper production of solid chocolate with more modern machines and Turin became the centre of artisanal chocolate. Venchi became famous for its Sigari di Cuba, Peyrano for its Alpino chocolates filled with liqueur, Baratti & Milano for its Nocciolatino – bitter chocolate covering two whole hazelnuts, Silvio Bessone for its Salame del Re and a handful of others. *Cioccolatini* became the fashionable way to eat chocolate, which up to then had only been a drink – a very fashionable drink favoured by the aristocracy and the higher echelons of society.

In the shops the assortment is bewildering, but the most popular Turinese chocolates are the *gianduiotti* and the *boeri*. Both these chocolates achieve such perfection of taste by combining extremely good chocolate with two great Piedmontese products. In the best *gianduiotti* the hazelnuts used are the Tonda Gentile delle Langhe variety, which grow in the provinces of Cuneo and Asti at a height of 300 to 700 metres. The nuts are hard and solid, with a delicate aroma, and have a very thin skin which is easily removed in the toasting. The *boeri* consist of a cherry preserved in alcohol, dipped into melted bitter chocolate. The very best *boeri* contain a Bella di Garbagna cherry, a very hard and crunchy fruit that keeps its bite very well when preserved.

Higher up in the mountains there are magnificent sweet chestnut trees, some of which produce the large chestnuts called *marroni*, used for *marrons glacés*. The first *marrons glacés* are said to have been made in Piedmont, after which they were made in France, now the largest producer. But are they the best? I dare say that the *marrons glacés* I recently ate in Turin were the best. Val and I bought some of them loose – and juicy – by weight and ate them in the hotel, like greedy children. I might be partial, but Val agreed that they were the best ever.

But it is not only chocolates and *marrons glacés* that will make your mouth water when you walk round one of the patisseries in Piedmont. There are also trays of *paste*, those little cakey things that range from *bignole* (sort of profiteroles) to *cannoncini* – small puff-pastry cannelloni filled with custard – and then further along to large cakes like the *torta gianduia* and the *torta di nocciole*, both made with the same hazelnuts as the *gianduiotti*, and at the end the parade of biscuits. There are *baci di dama* and *brutti ma buoni* and *pastine di meliga* – corn biscuits made with a variety of corn called Otto File which has an extremely sweet flavour; and *krumiri* in their old-fashioned tin and *canestrelli d' Ivrea* and *torcettoni* – all biscuits that the Piedmontese love to dunk in their *zabaglione* or eat with their *panna cotta* or with their *bônet*, a pudding from Alba made with *amaretti*, chocolate, eggs and a soupçon of rum, with the odd name – bonnet – due to its shape.

If I were to be asked which of all the Italian regions is the sweet tooth's paradise, I would without hesitation say 'Piedmont'.

Brutti ma Buoni

'Ugly but good' Hazelnut Biscuits

MAKES APPROX 50

4 large egg whites
250g/8oz caster sugar

250g/8oz hazelnuts, lightly toasted
and coarsely ground

Preheat the oven to 160°C/325°F/Gas Mark 3. Beat the egg whites until stiff, adding the sugar a little at a time. Stir in the ground hazelnuts. Put the mixture into a heatproof bowl over a pan of simmering water. Cook the mixture, stirring continuously for about 15 minutes. The mixture will become thick and will decrease in volume. Line baking sheets with baking paper. With a teaspoon, spoon small heaps of the mixture onto the lined trays and bake in the oven for 30–50 minutes. The biscuits should have dried out on the outside and become light golden in colour. Cool and store in an airtight tin.

Zabaglione di Nonna Rosetta

PER PERSON

1 tablespoon caster sugar
1 egg yolk

Marsala, premium quality

Crack the egg, reserving the eggshell to use as a measure. Using an electric whisk, beat the egg yolk in a heatproof bowl with the sugar to make a smooth, soft cream. Add ½ eggshell (4 teaspoons) of Marsala for each egg yolk and place the bowl over a pan of simmering water (do not let the bowl touch the water), whisking continuously without letting the mixture reach the boil. After about 10 minutes when the mixture becomes thick and foamy the *zabaglione* is ready. Serve immediately, as it will separate if left standing..

For a more delicate version, use Moscato d'Asti wine (in the same proportions) instead of Marsala.

Monte Bianco

SERVES 6

1kg/2lb 4oz large, round, fresh chestnuts
a little hot milk
75g/3oz sugar

50g/2oz unsweetened cocoa powder
1–2 tablespoons spoons of rum
300ml/½pt whipping cream,
    whipped and sweetened to taste

Boil the chestnuts for 1½ hours in plenty of water, topping it up as necessary so that the chestnuts are always covered. Check that the chestnuts are soft inside, and let them cool for about 30 minutes.

Peel the chestnuts whilst still warm, carefully removing all the fine inner brown skin. Purée them in a vegetable mill or food processor, and if the texture seems dry add a little milk. Add the sugar, the cocoa and the rum, stirring continuously until the mixture becomes smooth and soft. Taste and add more sugar and cocoa if necessary. Push the mixture through a mouli or a fine sieve letting it fall onto a serving plate in a mountain shape. The dough will look like long decorative strings.

Cover the mountain lightly with a generous amount of whipped cream and refrigerate before serving. Dust with a little cocoa powder just before serving.

Veneto

'In Venice even the ordinary sole
and the ugly great skate are striped
with delicate lilac lights, the
sardines shine like newly minted
silver coins, pink Venetian scampi
are fat and fresh, infinitely
entrancing in the early dawn.'
Elizabeth David, *Italian Food*

The cooking of this region is similar in all its seven provinces. This is due mainly to the influence that Venice, the Serenissima – the Most Serene – has had on all its territory. Having said that, I should add that for me there is one cuisine that stands slightly apart, and that is the cooking of Venice itself. This is a result of the great influence its overseas dominions had on the local cooking. Spices, for instance, are used in Venice with more liberality than in the *entroterra* – the hinterland. Meat is combined with fruit in dishes that speak of their Middle Eastern origins. Even table manners in Venice felt the influence of the oriental-Byzantine civilization. Massimo Alberini, the great gastronomic historian of the twentieth century, wrote in his *Antica Cucina Veneziana* that the two-pronged fork – the *piron* – was introduced to Venice by the Byzantine princess Theodora Ducas, the wife of the Doge Domenico Silvo, at the end of the eleventh century.

The other strong influence on the cooking of Venice was Jewish. Some Jews from Germany were allowed into Venice as moneylenders at the end of the fourteenth century, but most of the Jews who took refuge in Venice came when they were expelled from Spain and Portugal in 1492 and later from Sicily and southern Italy, which were under the control of Spain. Venice took the Jews in, and quite a few Jewish dishes became part of Venetian everyday food. *Bigoli in salsa* (see page 83) originated in the ghetto, as did spinach with pine nuts and

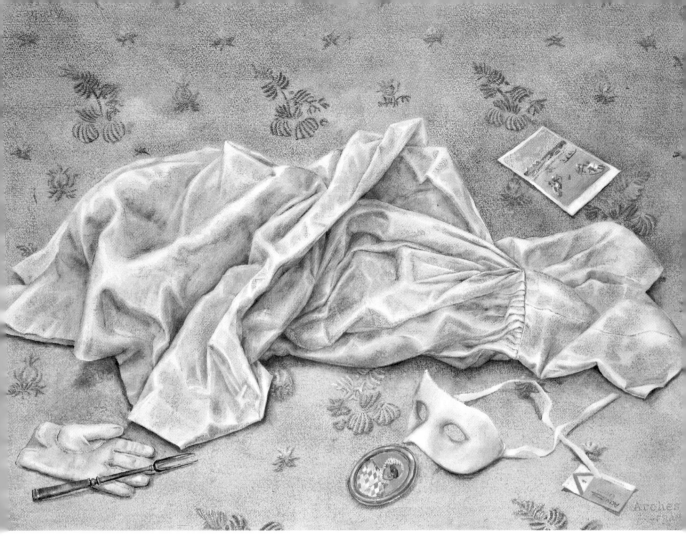

sultanas and *sformato di zucca* – pumpkin pudding. Preserved goose and all its *salami* and *prosciutti* always appear in any Venetian antipasto spread.

In Venice, more than in the hinterland, there are also all the dishes based on fish and seafood and crustaceans and everything fishy from the Adriatic, the *laguna* and the *valli*. These *valli*, found only around Venice, are neither open sea nor *laguna*, but shallow ponds of salt water separated from the sea by gates that can be opened to change the water and allow the intake of new fish. The *valli* were the original fish farms, as fish have been farmed in them for centuries. I was talking about this with fisherman Giuseppe Ranier, who took us out to see his *moleche* (see page 68). He confirmed that these *valli* indeed existed in Roman times, the difference between them and the modern fish farm being that in the *valli* the fish feed only on natural food.

The markets in Rialto and Chioggia are the best places to enjoy the diversity of sea creatures caught in the northern Adriatic. But of all fish, *baccalà* is without doubt the most popular. In Veneto *baccalà* is not salt cod, but stockfish. The Veneti prepare it in many ways, the two best known of which are *baccalà mantecato* and *baccalà alla vicentina* (see page 76), which is always served with polenta to mop up the onion and anchovy sauce.

There are three foods that unite Venice and Veneto: polenta, *baccalà* and rice. Rice is popular all over the Pianura Padana – the Po valley – from east of Turin to Venice, but it is in Veneto that it finds its *apogee* in its combination with all sorts of other ingredients – vegetables, fish, offal, crustaceans, cephalopods, etc. The Veneti say they have 365 ways of preparing a rice dish, one for every day of the year. When I'm in a restaurant in Veneto, and hear foreign visitors ordering a dish of spaghetti, I want to tell them, 'Please, eat spaghetti when you're in Naples or Palermo, but here have a wonderful risotto or a minestra di fagioli – bean soup.'

Like rice, beans are a popular food anywhere in Italy, but the borlotti beans you get in Veneto are the best, and of all the borlotti it is those from Lamon which come top. Lamon is a place in a pre-Dolomite valley. A few summers ago we were motoring down to Feltre with some friends when I spotted the name Lamon at the side of the road. I shouted 'Stop!' and stop we did. I wanted to see the place that gives its name to my favourite borlotti beans. It was just a common or garden mountain town situated in a rather narrow valley in the province of Belluno. But the origins of these beans are very aristocratic.

Beans were brought to Europe from America by the Spaniards. The sixteenth-century Pope Clement VII, Giulio de' Medici, was given seeds by a Spanish cardinal and he, in turn, gave them to a certain Piero Valeriano, an essayist from Belluno. Valeriano had the seeds sown in his land in Lamon and the American beans found there the ideal soil and climate to become the best borlotti. I have had many Lamon beans in the various *bacari* in Venice, where we had quite a few lunches during the years when we had a flat in Cannaregio. They are large beans, with a very thin skin and the most bean-tasting soft pulp. In the *bacari* they sit on the counter next to the tentacles of boiled octopus, the fried sardines *in saor*, all the different *cape* (scallops), *peoci* (mussels, stuffed or not), and other *cicheti* (snacks), all of which make a *bacaro* the best

OPPOSITE: *Borlotti beans and Venetian beads*

place in the world for a light lunch, accompanied, as it should be, by an *ombra* – a glass of wine.

There's not much proper meat in Veneto but there are plenty of birds and game, especially in the hinterland around Padua and Verona. And there's plenty of *baccalà* and lots of vegetables, Veneto being one of the biggest vegetable gardens of the peninsula.

Veneto produces more milk than any other Italian region, except for Lombardy. Hence the production of cheese is remarkable. And of all the traditional Veneto cheeses I love the Asiago, which comes from the plateau of the same name. I ate it there once, a cheese made in mountain huts from the milk of cows which were just there during the summer, high up in the foothills of the Alps. I prefer my Asiago fresh, as I do all cheeses. But there is also a semi-aged and an aged Asiago, as there is Montasio and the rare Vezzena and of course ricotta, either fresh or smoked.

Gnocchi di Patate con Zucchero e Cannella

Potato Dumplings with Sugar and Cinnamon

The dressing of these potato gnocchi is typical of the area south of Veneto and this recipe was given to us by the Trattoria Fiorluce in Camisano Vicentino. In Venice it is traditional to prepare these gnocchi on the feast of San Michele.

SERVES 4–5

1kg/2lb 4oz potatoes
250g/8oz Italian '00' flour
30g/1½oz Parmesan cheese, grated
salt

freshly grated nutmeg
unsalted butter
sugar
ground cinnamon

Peel the potatoes, cut them in pieces and cook them in boiling salted water until tender. Mash them with the flour, Parmesan, salt and a grating of nutmeg and set aside for 10 minutes. Shape the mixture into dumplings and drop them into boiling salted water – when they come to the surface and float, they will be ready. Drain and put into a hot serving dish. Dot them with butter and serve them very hot, with sugar and cinnamon sprinkled on top.

FARMYARD ANIMALS

When you look through any Veneto cookery book you will see relatively few recipes for beef, pork or lamb, some for offal, among which the always present *fegato alla veneziana* – liver with onions – and at least one for horsemeat. This will be for *pastissada de cavalo*, of which the best-known version hails from Verona, with an intriguing historic origin. When King Teodorico of the Visigoths defeated Odoacre in the fifth century in a battle near Verona, he told the starving people that they could go and help themselves to the horses killed in the battle. So the Veronesi created the *pastissada de cavalo*. I wonder whether the French created a good dish after the battle of Agincourt, though I doubt whether the English did after the battle of Hastings or indeed the Unionists after the battle of Getttysburg. If they did, Scarlett O'Hara would certainly have relished it.

Most of the *secondi piatti* – main course – recipes in Veneto are for fish, mainly *baccalà* (page 76) and for farmyard animals. There are recipes for duck, with or without stuffing, for capon, for guinea fowl, for goose both roasted and preserved, for turkey (a lovely recipe with pomegranate which sounds very Middle Eastern, see page 66), for pigeons and squabs, for young roasted peahens, for *osei* – little birds of any description – and, of course, for chickens, cockerels, poussins and old boilers to make stock. Many of the birds are simply roasted, usually accompanied by the piquant *peverada* sauce.

There is one bird that is bred and raised only in Veneto and that is the *gallina padovana* – the chicken from Padua – which is now a Slow Food Presidium. The *gallina padovana* claims a noble and exotic origin. The Marquis Giacomo Dondi dell'Orologio, during a visit to Poland in the fourteenth century, decided to bring back some crested Polish hens as ornamental birds for his gardens. The *padovana* hen does indeed look very much like the Polish one, although larger. By the twentieth century a few farmers were raising *padovana* hens. But in the gastronomically disastrous '60s they almost disappeared, until about fifteen years ago when they were resurrected by Slow Food.

We went to one of the farms where the *galline padovane* are raised, the Agriturismo Papaveri e Papere, near Padua, to meet the man responsible for the Presidium, Dr Gianni Brera, and the farmer, who showed us round his farm. The *gallina padovana* is a very odd-looking bird. It comes in five different colours – black, white, silver, gold or pale brown – and has a rich headdress of long feathers falling over its eyes, like a blown-up chrysanthemum. It is not a cosy bird at all; it looks like an over-made-up middle-aged woman who tries hard to still look young and sexy.

One of the birds was quite startling in appearance: it was a large bird with black and white feathers that made a whirly pattern all over its body. It looked as though it was exhibiting a new creation by the early twentieth-century dress designer Paul Poiret.

However odd the birds look, they are excellent in the pot, with their thin skin and their succulent brown flesh, similar to pheasant. The flavour is delicate yet assertive. They can be roasted, of course, but the classic recipe for a *padovana* is '*a la canevera*'. The chicken is stuffed with dessert apples, mixed with the juice and the zest of lemons and oranges and

with plenty of spices, a stuffing which in its sweet and sour flavour is redolent of the Venetian cuisine. Then it is pushed into a pig's bladder which is tied up around a bamboo stick – the *canevera* – to allow the steam to escape. It is boiled in a lot of water for about two and a half hours, with the result that the liquid in the bladder is a quintessential consommé. Cut into joints, the chicken is served with this juice and a little grated horseradish. Sadly I cannot pass any comment on the dish, as I've never tasted it.

Apart from the *galline padovane* at the Papaveri e Papere farm, there were all the other farmyard animals. The other chickens I saw for the first time were the *gallina collo nudo*, strange-looking birds with featherless necks, not very pretty, but apparently good in the pot. And there were lots of turkeys, squabs and guinea fowl strolling elegantly around.

There were also two or three peahens strutting around, certainly not as decorative as their male companions, but the ones to be enjoyed at table when just a few months old, roasted with *peverada*. A little farther on there were rabbit hutches and, in a field nearer to the house, four white kids, so lively and joyful and enchanting. Even I, the down-to-earth Latin, felt a pang of sorrow when I was told that they would be ready for Easter lunch, when kid is the traditional fare. I would have liked to buy one and bring it back to my garden in Dorset to amble happily around and munch the rich pasture of this green and pleasant land.

Faraona in Peverada

Guinea Fowl in Pomegranate Sauce

Pomegranate is fruit used at times in Venetian cooking which has a lot of Middle Eastern influence. This recipe has been adapted from the Slow Food book of the *Osterire del Veneto*.

SERVES 4

1 x 1.5kg/3lb 4oz guinea fowl
2 sprigs of fresh sage
2 sprigs of fresh rosemary
150ml/5fl oz white wine
juice of 2 pomegranates, reserving
  2 tablespoons of seeds

olive oil
1 onion, chopped
400g/14oz chicken livers, chopped
110g/4oz salami, chopped
juice of 1 lemon
salt and freshly ground black pepper

Preheat the oven to 200°C/400°F/Gas Mark 6. Cut the guinea fowl in quarters and put it into a roasting tray with the sage and rosemary. Pour over the wine and pomegranate juice and roast in the preheated oven for 45 minutes, until tender.

Heat a little olive oil in a pan and add the onion, livers and salami. Cook until the onion is soft and golden. Add the lemon juice. When the guinea fowl is cooked, remove it from the oven to a serving dish and keep warm. Add the juices from the roasting tray to the sauce in the pan, add the pomegranate seeds, season with salt and plenty of pepper, and leave to simmer for a few minutes. Serve with the guinea fowl.

MOLECHE, GRANCEVOLE, BACCALÀ, ET AL

It was the end of January, a beautiful warm sunny day, when I rang Luigi Boscolo to see if the *moleche* were ready. 'Si, signora,' he answered, 'and the fisherman will meet you in Chioggia in front of the Duomo.' But first things first. What are *moleche*? *Moleche* are common crabs caught at the time when they shed their carapace to form the new one. There are crabs everywhere in the Mediterranean, but it is only in the Venetian lagoon that they are caught in nets, selected, put into special containers called *vieri* and left there until they shed their carapace. They then become *moleche*, ready for the table.

Val and I went out on a boat with the fisherman Giuseppe Renier and his partner Armando Balla. On that beautiful spring-like day Chioggia looked at its best, with its thousands of boats lolling in the harbour. We were lucky, Giuseppe said, because due to the very warm winter the crabs were already *in muta* – changing. He picked out a few crabs that were just coming out of their shells. We could see how big the body was compared to the shell. In only a few hours the outside layer of the body would become hard again. The *muta* happens twice a year – in spring and autumn – and it is the skill of the fisherman to choose the right specimens, put them in the right container at the right time and then take them out *au point*, when they are ready to be eaten.

I have eaten *moleche* a few times, always fried after being coated in batter or flour. I prefer them in batter. When you eat them you bite the crust and sink your teeth into a soft morsel of condensed sea. Heaven! One recipe is particularly interesting: *moleche col pien* – stuffed *moleche*. The live *moleche* are put into a basin containing beaten eggs, salt and grated Parmesan. The poor little beasts feast on the beaten eggs for a few hours and then, when they are sluggish from over-eating, they are coated with flour and fried.

Frying is certainly the most popular way of cooking small fish such as sardines, hake, gobies and small cephalopods. It keeps the fresh taste of the fish intact within its golden crust. Grilling is used for larger fish such as daurade or sea bass, and boiling for all crustaceans, from the precious *grancevola* or spider crab to the poor man's *canocchia* – mantis shrimp.

Grancevola is one of the best antipasti you can have in Venice. Once boiled, it is opened and the chopped meat and coral are served in the upper shell, lightly dressed with olive oil and a little lemon juice, salt and pepper. There is a recipe which is said to have been found in the diary of the Austrian general Count Radetzky, a successful marriage between the cooking of Venice and that of Vienna. The *grancevola* meat is mixed with béchamel, Parmesan and egg yolk. Flavoured with brandy and Worcester sauce, it is spooned into the upper shell and baked for five minutes. Interesting, but I'm sure the simple Venetian recipe is far better.

The other popular crustaceans are the scallops, of which the little *canestrelli* are the tastiest, perfect for a risotto and even better floured and fried. Mussels, again, are perfect for a risotto or a soup. Eel is more popular in Venice than elsewhere in Italy. There are two well-known recipes, *bisato alla Veneziana* – breaded, fried in oil, then flavoured with vinegar or Marsala – and *bisato su l'ara* – an intriguing recipe from Murano in which the cut-up eel is baked between two layers of bay leaves.

And now to the most popular of all fish, *baccalà*, which is what the Veneti call stockfish, that nasty-smelling, woody stick of a fish which they are able to transform into succulent delicious food. Stockfish has always been popular in Venice, so much so that in 1827 a Norwegian firm established a large storeroom there which was a great help to the Venetians during the Austrian siege of 1849, when *baccalà* and, it is said, cats kept them alive.

After a preliminary soaking of at least three days, the *baccalà* is fried, or dressed in a sweet and sour sauce, or stewed in tomato sauce, or roasted, just to mention the recipes that first come to my mind. But the two outstanding recipes from Veneto are *baccalà alla vicentina* (page 76) and *baccalà mantecato*, in which the *baccalà*, boiled in water or milk and flavoured with plenty of garlic, is *mantecato* – beaten while adding olive oil very slowly, as for a mayonnaise. The secret of a good *baccalà mantecato* is to be able to make the *baccalà* absorb a good deal of oil by beating it hard with a wooden spoon.

While we were talking about *baccalà*, Giuseppe Ercole told me that when he was a boy, the only way he liked his *baccalà mantecato* was dipped in a bowl of salsa rossa. His father used to send this sauce to him regularly, together with the salsa verde while he was away at boarding school, and these kept at bay his homesickness for the traditional fare of his region, Piedmont.

Fish, and *baccalà*, is always served with polenta, preferably white polenta, the perfect accompaniment. So perfect, indeed, that there is a saying in Venetian dialect: 'We must make a monument to the person who invented *polenta e baccalà*.'

Frittata di Moleche

Moleche *Omelette*

This recipe is from Armanda Vinello, Venice. The delicious soft crabs are mixed with eggs for one of the best *frittate* I have ever tasted.

SERVES 4

500g/1lb 2oz **moleche**
Italian '00' flour, enough to
    coat the **moleche**
oil for deep frying

4 eggs
salt and freshly ground black pepper
olive oil or a knob of unsalted butter

Clean, wash and dry the *moleche*. Dip them into the flour and fry them in very hot oil for 3–4 minutes per side. Cut them into big pieces. Beat the eggs in a large bowl with a little salt and pepper. Add the *moleche* pieces and stir well.

Heat a little oil (or a knob of butter) in a frying pan. When the oil is hot, pour in the mixture and allow to cook, shaking the pan every now and again. Turn the omelette over, take the pan off the heat and serve immediately.

'The colour of Venetian foods, seen in the soft light of Venetian skies, no doubt inspired Venetian cooks, while Venetian wealth gave them the means to delight the palate as well as the eye.'
Waverley Root, *The Food of Italy*

OVERLEAF: *Fortuny fabric and moleche*

Risotto Nero

Black Risotto

Giuseppe Maffioli is the greatest authority on Venetian food and his book – *La Cucina Veneziana* – is certainly the best on this fascinating subject.

SERVES 6

2 tablespoons olive oil

1 onion, finely sliced

1 garlic clove, finely sliced

1kg/2lb 4 oz small cuttlefish, cleaned,
   with their ink sacks intact

salt and freshly ground black pepper

½ glass white wine

300g/10 oz risotto rice

1 litre/1¾ pints fish stock

a knob of unsalted butter

a handful of grated Parmesan cheese

Heat the oil in a pan and add the onion and garlic. Cook gently until soft and golden. Add the cuttlefish and season with salt and pepper. Let the cuttlefish cook very slowly for 30 minutes, then add the wine and continue cooking to let the alcohol evaporate. Add the rice and then, whilst stirring, gradually add the fish stock and the ink from the sack until the rice is cooked. Turn the heat off, stir in the butter and Parmesan, and serve.

Sarde in Saor

Sardines in Sweet and Sour Sauce

At harvest time the women used to take this dish to their men working in the fields, along with *polenta abbrustolita* (roasted polenta). This recipe comes from the Osteria Al Bacco, in Venice.

SERVES 4–5

1kg/2lb 4oz sardines, cleaned
Italian '00' flour, enough to coat
*   the sardines*
olive oil, for frying
1kg/2lb 4oz onions

300ml/½ pint white vinegar
50g/2oz raisins
25g/1oz pine nuts
salt and freshly ground black pepper

Roll the sardines in flour and shake off the excess. Fry them in very hot oil for a few minutes, then drain them on kitchen paper and sprinkle with salt.

Meanwhile put the onions into a separate pan with about 4cm/1¾ inches of water and simmer gently until soft. When the onions are nearly ready, add the vinegar, a little oil and the raisins and mix together. Cook together for about 30 seconds, but don't let the onions brown. Arrange alternate layers of sardines and onions in a serving dish and scatter over the pine nuts and season with salt and pepper.

This dish is best eaten the day after it is made. Stored in a cool, dry place, it can be kept for more than a week.

'Bring me some sardines, but see that you choose the best ones. The ones on top are always the best. When they are tired they have a red head.'
Carlo Goldoni, *Le Donne di Casa Sua*

Baccalà alla Vicentina

Stockfish from Vicenza

Another recipe from the book *La Cucina Veneziana* by Giuseppe Maffioli.

SERVES 6

1kg/2lb 4oz stockfish or salt cod, soaked
50g/2oz unsalted butter
olive oil
4 garlic cloves, finely chopped
a small bunch of parsley, finely chopped
salt and freshly ground black pepper

1 onion, chopped
1 litre/1¾ pints milk
a pinch of cinnamon
110g/4oz Parmesan cheese, grated
50g/2oz anchovy fillets, chopped

Preheat the oven to 190°C/375°F/Gas Mark 5. Cut the fish into even-sized pieces. Melt the butter with a drizzle of olive oil in an ovenproof frying pan and add half the garlic and half the parsley. Cook for a few minutes, then add the fish to the pan and cook gently until golden. Add the onion, then season the fish with salt and pepper, cover it with milk and sprinkle with cinnamon. Bring to the boil, cover the pan, and lower the heat, leaving it to simmer until the milk has almost all been absorbed. Sprinkle with the Parmesan.

Turn the pieces of fish over and sprinkle with the rest of the parsley and garlic and the anchovies. Drizzle with olive oil. Put the pan into the preheated oven for 10 minutes and serve hot with polenta.

LA POLENTA

Of all Italian staples, the one that we Italians most associate with Veneto is polenta, yellow or white, soft or hard, grilled or fried, the comfort food that has kept the Veneti happy since maize first arrived at Rialto from America in the sixteenth century. 'Maize growing is thought to have been introduced in Venetia in 1539 and had spread to the entire Terra Firma sometime between the end of the century and the beginning of the next one,' wrote the great Fernand Brandel in his *The Structure of Everyday Life*.

Polenta made with all sorts of other cereals, from millet to buckwheat, had always been part of the daily food of the Veneti. And when maize was first planted in Veneto the result was miraculous. Tall strong shoots carrying beautiful cobs were sprouting everywhere, even in the marshes of Polesine, and the locals could at last no longer feel the hunger that had haunted them for centuries. It was an easy plant to grow, with a rich yield.

By the end of the seventeenth century, however, a strange new disease became evident, characterized by skin lesions, weakness and, in extreme cases, mental degeneration. Because of the skin lesions the disease was called pellagra – rough skin. So rife was it that in 1786 Goethe wrote in his *Italian Journey*, 'Their features spoke of misery and their children looked pitiful ... I believe this unhealthy condition is due to their constant diet of maize and buckwheat or, as they call them, yellow and black polenta.' Believing this to be the case, polenta was banned and people, yet again, starved. It was only much later that the cause of pellagra was discovered. It was not what the people were eating but rather what they were not eating. Consuming only polenta, as so many did in the winter, the Veneti's diet was deficient in essential nutrients and vitamins. Once that was discovered, polenta became popular again, as it still is. And now it is the traditional peasant food that has become the fodder of the great and the good.

Although nowadays quite a few Italians still make polenta in their beautiful copper *paiolo* – the polenta pot that looks like a squat bucket – in the old-fashioned way, which takes a good three-quarters of an hour of standing and stirring, most people who regularly make polenta have an electric paddle that paddles the flour around in the *paiolo*. You just switch it on and leave the kitchen. Easy and efficient. Of course there is on the market *polenta istantanea*, a pre-cooked polenta that cuts the cooking time down to five minutes. Not bad. However, the flavour is certainly not as good, and unfortunately it is the most common polenta flour sold outside Italy. But since I do not possess an electric paddle nor, frankly, am I prepared to stand by the cooker for three-quarters of an hour with a long stick in my hand to stir the yellow mass, nor do I like to eat *polenta istantanea* if I can help it, I do something else. I was given the recipe by my mentor, the great gastronomic historian of the last century, Massimo Alberini, who was born in Padua and lived in Venice and Milan. (You will find it on page 81.)

Massimo told me a lot about Veneto and polenta and I first learnt from him that the Veneti are divided into two factions: the white polenta faction and the yellow polenta faction. When I was recently in Veneto I asked quite a few people which polenta they preferred and almost everybody had definite opinions and likings. Most people said that white polenta is the right polenta to eat with fish, though some went on to say that they preferred white polenta with everything. But I also met a few 'yellow polenta with everything' fans who, very humbly, admitted that they were in the wrong. In our house in Milan we used the yellow polenta of Lombardy, the polenta my father liked, but at the house of my maternal grandparents, who were both from Veneto, I remember having that lovely soft ivory stuff which I much preferred.

Val and I went to Castelfranco Veneto to talk to Professor Renato Ballan, who is in charge of the Slow Food Presidium of the *mais biancoperla* – pearl white maize, which is indeed the colour of the lovely cobs. Professor Ballan told us that up to the Second World War, in the provinces of Venice, Treviso and Rovigo, polenta was always white. After the war it nearly disappeared to make way for the more productive hybrid varieties. Some fifteen years ago the Regione del Veneto decided to reinstate the ancient *biancoperla* and, with the help of the Strampelli Research Institute, it is now successfully cultivated by a group of keen farmers around Treviso. So *polenta bianca* is triumphantly back on the plates of the discerning connoisseurs who appreciate its delicacy and full flavour.

The production of this flour is extremely costly. The cobs are harvested by hand and the grains are also removed by hand. I tried to detach a grain from the cob in front of me. Impossible. 'Oh no, not with your fingers, but with a strong pointed tool – a *spunzon*,' Professor Ballan said. The grains are all ground by millstones driven by water. The whole performance is well worth it, as we realized later at lunch when we had some *polentina bianca* with our *pesce fritto*. I was highly amused that Professor Ballan, in spite of being responsible for the Slow Food Presidium, prefers yellow polenta for the simple reason that it is what his father liked – a reminder of my own childhood – while Lucio Torresan, who was our Radicchio di Treviso man, said that he only eats white polenta. 'Perfect with radicchio,' (see page 83) he said, adding, 'That's what my father liked.'

Polenta is still eaten frequently in Veneto – at least twice a week – thanks to its ability to be matched successfully to so many different ingredients: meat, fish, cheese or vegetables. Polenta is so happy with everything that in the province of Cuneo, in Piedmont, it has gained the soubriquet of 'La Traviata', since, like Violetta, it adapts very easily to different partners.

Bigoli in Salsa all' Ebraica

Bigoli with Jewish Sauce

Jewish cuisine had a great influence on Venetiano cooking. Maffioli has written extensively on the subject and here is his recipe for *Bigoli in Salsa*. *Bigoli* are the thick-stranded pasta of the Veneto region.

SERVES 4

500g/1lb 2oz **bigoli**
1 glass of olive oil
12 anchovy fillets, chopped

2 garlic cloves, chopped
a large bunch of fresh parsley, chopped
freshly ground black pepper

Put a large pan of water on to boil and cook the *bigoli* until *al dente*. Heat the olive oil in a small pan and add the anchovies. Stir until they melt into the oil, then add the garlic and parsley and cook for 1 minute. Serve this sauce with the pasta, and sprinkle with plenty of pepper.

THE RED RADICCHIOS

There are four red radicchios of which three grow only in one region – Veneto – while the Radicchio di Chioggia is grown everywhere. It is a new variety, post Second World War, easy to produce but of relatively poor quality and rather despised by radicchio connoisseurs. It is the radicchio we can buy everywhere, at any time of the year. When I was in Castelfranco and I mentioned it, the answer was, 'But that is not real radicchio.' So, forget it. Here are the real radicchios.

The Radicchio rosso di Verona 'is of rounded shape, of red and brilliant rose colour, with a lighter heart and fragile ribs. It has a pleasant bitter flavour, but it cannot be used in many ways.' So wrote the late Count Giovanni Capnist in his book *La Cucina Veronese*. In the book Count Capnist gives a simple salad recipe for the Radicchio di Verona, which he dresses very suitably with extra virgin olive oil from Lake Garda and the juice of a lemon, also from Lake Garda, both outstanding but enjoyed, alas, only in situ. It is worth noting that the olive and lemon trees of Lake Garda flourish in this northern latitude with a climate that makes the olives less peppery and the lemons sweeter.

The Radicchio variegato di Castelfranco is like a beautiful cabbage rose of a greeny-ivory colour flecked with magenta spots – 'as if from the brush of Jackson Pollock', Val said. This radicchio can be used in the same way as its better-known cousin, the Radicchio rosso di Treviso. This latter is the star of all radicchios, and with that of Castelfranco was the first vegetable or fruit to be granted an IGP – indication of geographic protection.

Radicchio di Treviso is mostly cultivated in the Parco del Sile, a beautiful green oasis near Treviso, a part of Veneto where otherwise light industries have transformed the landscape for the worse, but have brought wealth to what was once a very deprived area. The Radicchio di Treviso, although it certainly existed long before, was first mentioned in local documents in the second half of the nineteenth century. It was then that its cultivation started and by the beginning of the twentieth century it had become an important part of the local agriculture. The seeds are sown in June and July, or small plants are transplanted in August, in fields where cereals have grown in the preceding year. The harvest starts on 1 November. The roots are cleaned and trimmed off, and the plants are gathered in bunches and immersed in a trough of spring waters of the river Sile and nearby rivulets, waters that have a steady temperature of 12–15°C. The plants stay there for 15–20 days, a period of time about which only the skill of the farmers can decide. The heart of each plant gradually grows, forming a flower, and reaches the desired length, while the leaves gain the desired crispness and bitterness.

This became quite clear when we went to the farm belonging to the Torresan family near Castelfranco. Lucio Torresan is the president of the Consorzio del Radicchio rosso di Treviso e variegato di Castelfranco. The whole family was at work that day, from Lucio's beautiful eighty-year-old mother, to his wife and his son and nephew, Paolo and Andrea, the actual owners of the farm, plus a few other helpers. They were all stripping the outside leaves off each radicchio, trimming the roots and gathering the plants in big bunches to be immersed in tanks in the hangars next door. Even Dante, the friendly mongrel, seems to take part in the work.

Lucio speaks of his radicchio with love and enthusiasm, obviously shared by all his family, as so often happens in Italy. He described to us the great *festa* which takes place in Treviso on the second weekend in December, when the main square, the beautiful Piazza dei Signori, is covered with bunches of *radicchio rosso*. This is the Festa del Radicchio in Campo, when the Piazza dei Signori looks like a field of giant spider-like red flowers whose long legs undulate in the wintry wind.

Radicchio del Signor Torresan

This recipe comes from
Signor Lucio Torresan,
President of the Consorzio del Radicchio.

'Cut some pancetta into small cubes (I suggest unsmoked *pancetta tesa*) and sauté in oil with 1 chopped onion. Add red vinegar and partly evaporate. Pour over the radicchio (Treviso or Castelfranco, but here let's use Castelfranco or Verona), cut in large strips.'

OPPOSITE: *Radicchio di Verona*

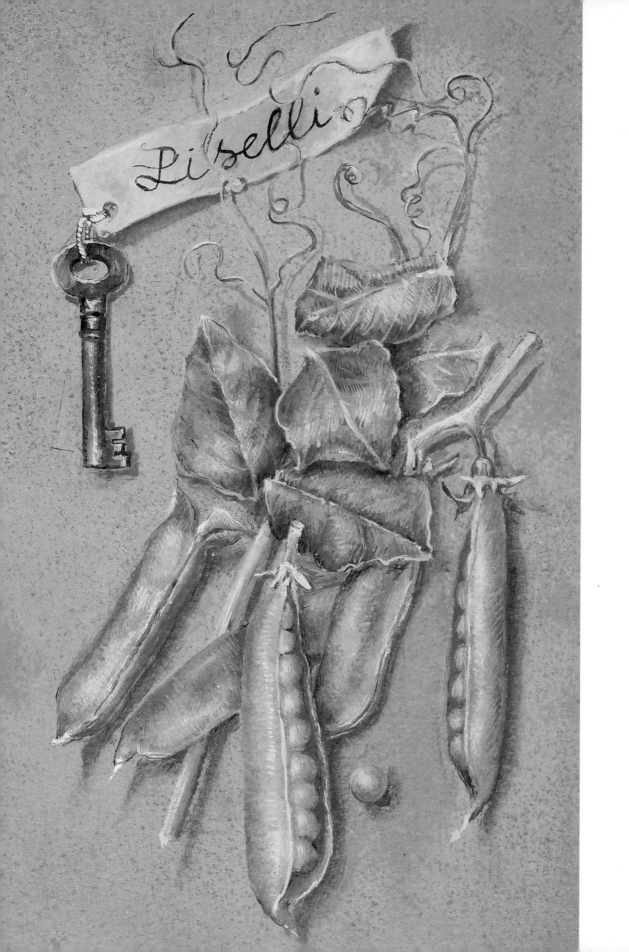

Risi e Bisi

Rice and Peas

Risi e Bisi is one of the classic dishes of Veneto. The recipe comes from *The Da Fiore Cookbook* by Damiano Martin, the son of the chef-patronne of the Da Fiore restaurant in Venice, one of the best restaurants in Italy.

SERVES 6

1.1kg/2½lbs fresh peas in their pods
3 litres/5 pints water
salt
3 tablespoons unsalted butter
2 tablespoons olive or sunflower oil
55g/2oz pancetta, diced
1 small onion, finely chopped

½ cinnamon stick
750g/1½lbs Carnaroli or Vialone Nano rice
½ bunch flat-leaf parsley leaves,
    finely chopped
5 tbsp freshly grated Parmesan, plus some
    for sprinkling
freshly ground black pepper

Shell the peas, reserving the pods. Place the pods in a medium saucepan with 3 litres of lightly salted water. Bring to a boil over a high heat, reduce the heat to medium-low and simmer, uncovered, for an hour. Strain the broth into a medium-sized pot, pressing on the pods. Discard the pods. Keep the broth warm over medium heat.

Melt a tablespoon of the butter and the oil into a large, heavy saucepan over medium heat. Add the pancetta and onion and cook, stirring until the onion is golden, about 10 minutes. Add the peas, cinnamon stick, and 8 tablespoons of broth. Cover and cook until the peas are tender, about 5 minutes.

Increase the heat to high, uncover and cook off any remaining liquid. Add the rice and stir well to coat. Add about 140ml/5fl oz warm broth and cook, stirring constantly until most of the broth has been absorbed. Add about 140ml/5fl oz more broth. Continue cooking, stirring and adding broth as needed until the rice is tender but firm to the bite, about 18 minutes. Remove from the heat and stir in just enough broth so that the rice is loose but not watery (*Risi e Bisi* should be slightly soupier than ordinary risotto). Stir in the remaining 2 tablespoons butter, the parsley and the Parmesan. Cover and allow to rest for a few minutes. Serve with additional Parmesan and sprinkle with black pepper.

THE VEGETABLES OF THE ISLANDS ON THE LAGOON

I was once flying from Bari to Munich. It was a spectacular day and, as I looked out of the window, there, just under our flight path, was a blue expanse of water with the islands of Venice and of the Giudecca and the Lido and with many smaller islands to the east. They looked like a myriad of brown drops fallen into that blue expanse from the brush of some heavenly painter. What happens in those half-forgotten places? Who lives there? And then I remembered, and in my mind's eye there appeared piles of small green artichokes, rows of purple and cream aubergines, bunches of courgette flowers and mountains of red watermelons, yellow melons and beans of all sizes and colours.

A few months later Val and I were on the Fondamenta Nove waiting to board the *vaporetto* for Sant'Erasmo, one of those brown drops I had seen from the sky. It was a bitterly cold January day. The icy cold Bora (or was it the Tramontana?) was blowing from the east or the north. The *vaporetto* was not heated, just warmed up by us and a handful of inhabitants of those forlorn islands of the lagoon, stamping up and down the cabin to keep warm. And then I remembered my previous journey to Sant'Erasmo. It was on a sultry July day, the kind of day that is unpleasant in most cities but which in Venice seems to bring out the pervading melancholy and mystery of the lagoon. The steeples, bell towers and cupolas of the churches seem to stand out more sharply against the misty background, with that kind of ethereal luminosity that has inspired Turner and so many other painters. But that January morning even the brush of a Turner could not have made the scenery appealing.

We got to Sant'Erasmo in a fierce flurry of icy snow and were greeted by a smiling young man on his bicycle. He was Carlo Finotello, the farmer with whom we were going to have a chat and a lunch at the Ristorante Ca'Vignotto, some 800 metres down the road. I said that no way would I walk those 800 metres in that weather; we could have our meeting in the church opposite. 'Wait a minute,' Carlo said, and rushed off, to reappear a few minutes later at the wheel of the oldest Panda imaginable – the priest's car. In coughs and spurts, we arrived at Ca'Vignotto and sat happily at the table in the warm restaurant with a cup of coffee and talked about vegetables and fruit before enjoying a lovely lunch cooked by Gabriella Zanella, the chef and owner.

Carlo is a third-generation farmer; I was amazed to meet a

young man working on the land. When I had been in Sant'Erasmo on that July day I had interviewed a much older farmer, a grower of aubergines, who told me that all the young men had left the islands and gone to work on the '*terra ferma*'. Carlo said that he and his brother have to thank Slow Food for the help they received in setting up the Presidium of the Carciofo Violetto di Sant'Erasmo, for which Carlo is responsible, and for inspiring them with the enthusiasm to carry on the hard work of their ancestors.

Carlo told me that it is the soil of the islands, salty, well-drained and limey, that produces such flavourful vegetables, and the fact that all the vegetable gardens on the islands are watered with fresh water, not the water of the lagoon. He talked a lot about his passion, the *castraure*, the small artichokes which are the prize product of Sant'Erasmo, and of the melons which are the other special produce. The *castraure* are the first *capolini* – heads – of the artichoke plants, and are removed from the plant in the spring to be sold in special markets such as Rialto, in shops such as Peck in Milan or the best restaurants.

There are quite a few islands on the lagoon, of which Sant'Erasmo is the largest, and all are dedicated to the cultivation of fruit and vegetables. The highly priced vegetables grown there are ready, for obvious climatic reasons, later than those of Sicily, Sardinia or even Liguria, which is blessed with a very mild climate. But they compete successfully and even win in flavour over those of the warmer regions. The Rialto market is the best place to see them displayed and to have a lesson in seasonality. In the spring the stalls are loaded with 'the first peas from Torcello' or 'the first *castraure* from Sant'Erasmo'. The next stall is a red mountain of the 'first tomatoes' and 'first courgettes' from Puglia or Sicily. And in between there are the smaller stalls of salads and herbs, with little mounds of *bruscandoli* (wild hops, so good in risotti), wild fennel, wild asparagus and other wild plants and herbs, plus heaps of bright green lamb's lettuce – the Easter salad, contrasting with the red of the last radicchio di Treviso. During the glorious days of the Serenissima the first peas of Torcello used to be given to the Doge. Now they probably go to Harry's Bar and other such restaurants. I only hope that the clients appreciate these delicacies, which are indeed fit for a Doge.

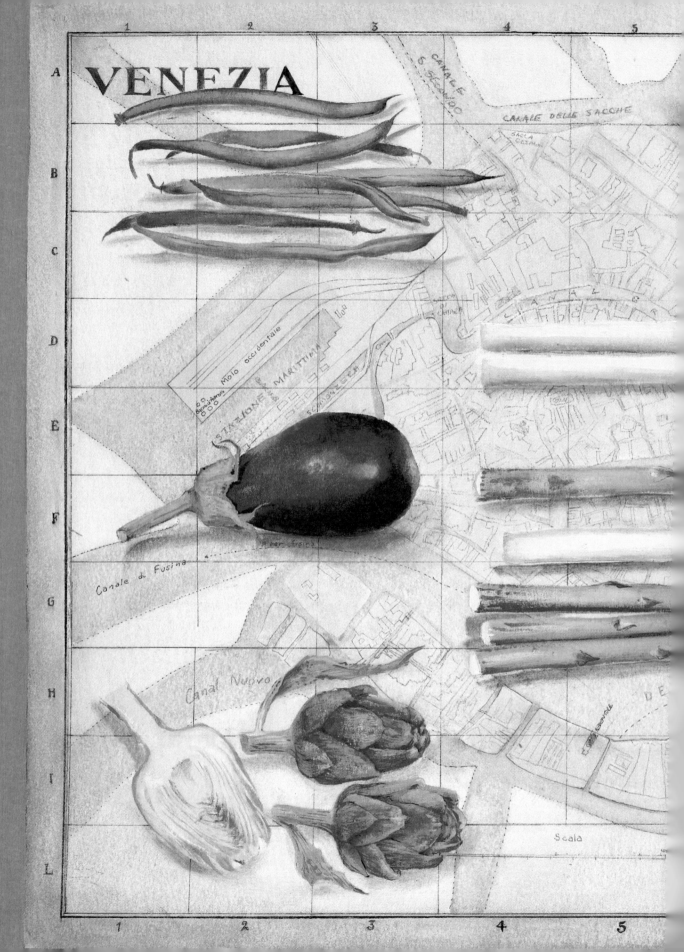

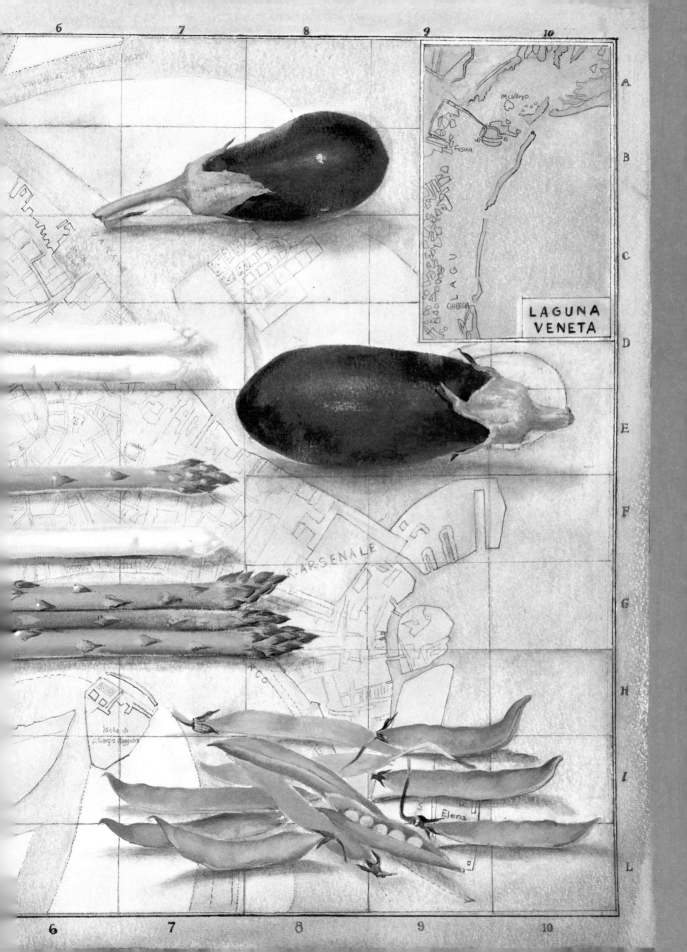

LAGUNA
VENETA

Zuppa di Fagioli e Orzo

Minestrone with Beans and Barley

We had this lovely soup at the ristorante La Bitta in Venice. It was so good I asked for the recipe.

SERVES 8–10

250g/8oz dried beans, preferably Lamon variety
1 large onion, chopped
2 carrots, chopped
2 garlic cloves, chopped
75g/3oz pancetta, chopped
2 bay leaves
2 sprigs of rosemary
1 litre/1¾ pints vegetable stock
100g/3½oz pearl barley
olive oil
salt and freshly ground black pepper

Soak the beans in cold water for at least 12 hours, then drain and put into a very large pan. Add the onion, carrot, garlic, pancetta, bay leaves and rosemary. Cover with vegetable stock and bring to the boil. Cook on a low heat for 40 minutes to 1 hour until the beans are tender.

Meanwhile cook the barley in boiling water for about 10 minutes and drain. When the beans are cooked, remove a third of them and reserve, and either put the rest through a vegetable mill or whizz in a blender. Add the barley and the reserved whole beans to the soup pan and continue cooking for 1 hour until the barley is tender. Season well with salt and pepper, sprinkle with a few drops of olive oil, and serve. The soup will be soft, creamy and thick.

PROSCIUTTO DI SAN DANIELE

'If the sea and the mountains could be moved, a *prosciutto* like this could be made anywhere.' That was a slogan I saw across a street in San Daniele when I went to have a look and a taste at the *festa del prosciutto*. San Daniele is a delightful town on top of a hill in Friuli-Venezia Giulia, not actually in Veneto but next door to it. The town is famous for one thing: its *prosciutti*, which are considered on a par with the *prosciutti di Parma*. And on the last weekend in June the *prosciutti* are rightly celebrated, as indeed they should be, with music and dancing and eating and drinking, with everybody sitting down at long trestle tables with a plate of pink *prosciutto*, a packet of breadsticks and a bottle of beer.

The *prosciutto di San Daniele* is in every way as good as that of Parma, with the difference that its production is far smaller – around a quarter less. There are now thirty producers, all of whom have their factories around the town itself. This is where the warm, humid breezes from the Adriatic meet the cold dry wind from the Alps, creating the ideal climate for drying

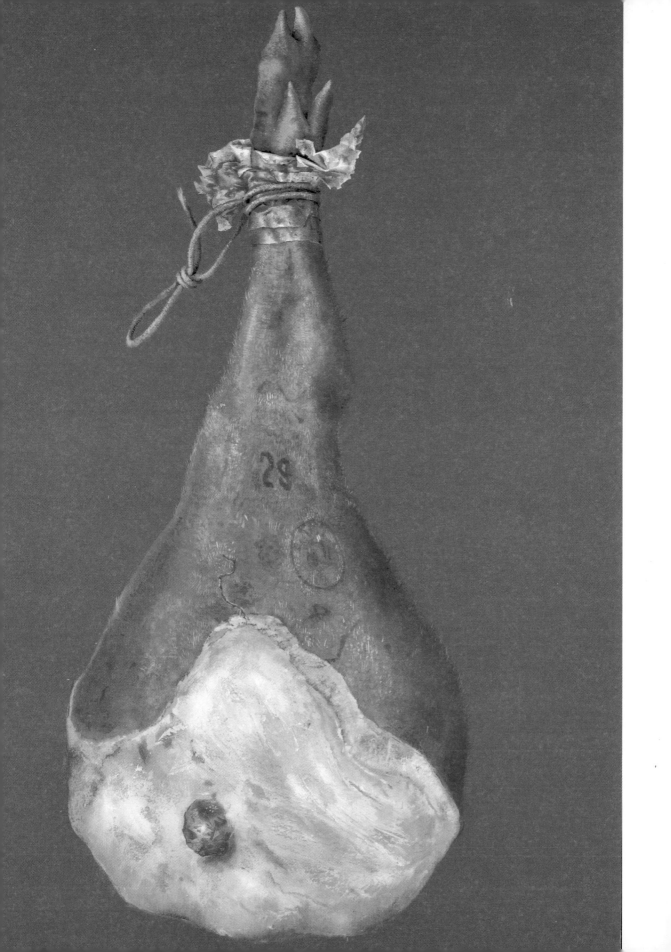

the *prosciutti*, similar to that found in Langhirano, the *prosciutto* town south of Parma.

I was shown round by one of the producers and treated to two delightful lunches of *prosciutto e melone* and a glass of chilled Tocai Friulano. At one of the lunches the *prosciutto* arrived with a large dish of *verdure sott' olio* – vegetables under oil: aubergines, peppers, courgettes, small onions and sun-dried tomatoes. I was told, 'Yes, you can eat them with *prosciutto*, although the purists prefer to eat the *prosciutto* first when the palate is fresh and more appreciative.' And this is what I did, preferring to be able to taste the *prosciutto* in all its glory; the vegetables afterwards were good too.

Prosciutti di San Daniele have been produced for years, but only in the 70s did the production become an important industry of the area. In the past the best twenty *prosciutti* were sent each year to the Doge in Venice so that the town of San Daniele could keep its independence from the Venetian Republic, which considered Friuli an area to be exploited. Later on, when Friuli-Venezia Giulia was under the Austro-Hungarian Empire, *prosciutti* were sent to the Hapsburgs in Vienna.

In 1797, during the Napoleonic invasion of northern Italy, one of the French generals was sent to San Daniele to take away 2,000 *prosciutti*. The story goes that almost exactly 200 years later, in 1979, the mayor of the town was making plans to ask President Jacques Chirac for the return of the *prosciutti*! The French had to give back to Venice the four bronze horses that Napoleon had stolen, but they are apparently still enjoying the 2,000 *prosciutti* of San Daniele.

When Lord Byron was in Venice he had a passionate affair with Margherita Cogni, the beautiful wife of a baker. She was a loud and ignorant woman, who is said to have kept slices of polenta between her breasts to keep it warm and to have it ready for the occasional bite. She was illiterate, a failing which Byron appreciated since, as he said, she would not be able to bore him with letters.

I DOLCI

SWEETS

One cannot write about the food of Veneto and ignore its *dolci*. After all, it was Venice that introduced sugar to Europe; oddly enough it was first called 'Indian salt'. In Padua there is a good cake called *pinza* made with yellow maize flour, enriched with sultanas, dried figs and fennel seeds and given a strong aroma by spices: ginger, cinnamon, nutmeg and cloves. All over Veneto there is the *fugassa* (dialect for *focaccia*), an ancient sweet bread which, when cooked, is covered with peeled almonds and sugar crystals, the traditional Easter food. The Venetians like to cut it into thin slices and dunk it in Malvasia wine. Of a much more modern date is the best-known Italian pud in absolute: *tiramisù*. It was created after the Second World War in Treviso at the *ristorante* El Toulà and became an immediate success.

But it is the small sweets , the biscuits and the fritters that are the strongest element in the sweet-making of the Veneto. Among these I must mention *zaleti*, biscuits made of maize flour and sultanas, and *baicoli*, very delicate thin biscuits which in the old days were dipped in the most fashionable drink, hot chocolate. Hot chocolate was allegedly first made in Italy by Florian in the eighteenth century and it soon became the 'in drink' of the great and the good. Coffee was already quite popular in Venice, as it arrived in 1649 – it was the first place in Europe to enjoy coffee. The first coffee shop opened in 1683 in Piazza San Marco and more followed quickly, including a shop founded in 1720 by Floriano Francesconi. Florian became, and still is, the best-known coffee house in the world.

The other two great sweets of Veneto are fritters and they are – or used to be – made at carnival time. One of these is *galani* (see page 101) and the other is *fritole*, balls made of a mixture of eggs, flour, yeast, sugar, wine and milk, studded with sultanas and pine nuts. The mixture is dropped by the spoonful into boiling oil. Nowadays *fritole* are also made with a plain mixture, filled with crème patissière or zabaglione. *Fritole*, or *frittelle*, are so closely associated with enjoyment and indulgence that the expression *fare le fritole* has, I have been told, become a euphemism for making love.

BAICOLI
FAMOSI BISCOTTI VENEZIANI
COLUSSI

I Bussolai

Venetian Biscuits

These lovely S-shaped biscuits originally came from the island of Burano but they are very popular in Venice and all over Veneto. This is the recipe from the Bussolai made by Gabriella Zanella at her Ristorante Ca' Vignotto on the island of Sant' Erasmo.

MAKES 60–70

12 egg yolks
1 egg white
600g/1lb 5oz caster sugar
300g/10oz unsalted butter, softened

1kg/2lb Italian '00' flour
grated zest of 1 unwaxed lemon
1 teaspoon vanilla extract
50ml/2fl oz rum

Preheat the oven to 180°C/350°F/Gas Mark 4. Put the egg yolks and egg white into a large bowl and add the sugar. Using an electric hand whisk, beat well until combined. Gradually add lumps of the softened butter until it is all combined, then gradually add the flour, lemon zest, vanilla extract and the rum until a stiff paste is formed (you may need to do this by hand if it is very stiff). Roll small handfuls of the mixture into balls the size of a walnut. On a floured board, roll into sausage shapes, then bend into 'S' shapes. Bake on baking sheets in the preheated oven for about 20 minutes, then leave to cool on a rack.

Galani

Galani

Another recipe from Damiano Martin's *The Da Fiore Cookbook*.

MAKES APPROX 60

2 large eggs

25g/1oz sugar

pinch salt

30ml/1fl oz olive oil

30ml/1fl oz rum

½ teaspoon pure vanilla extract

grated zest of ½ unwaxed lemon

250g/8oz plain flour

1 teaspoon baking powder

2 litres/3½ pints corn or sunflower oil

icing sugar, for dusting

In a large bowl, beat together the eggs, sugar and salt. Whisk in the oil, then the rum, vanilla and lemon zest. Using a wooden spoon, mix in the flour and baking powder. Once the dough comes together, turn it out onto a work surface lightly dusted with flour and knead until it is smooth and uniform; continue to dust with flour to prevent it sticking. Place in a bowl, cover and set aside for 3 hours to relax the dough.

Cut the dough into quarters and roll them through a pasta machine, one by one until you reach the finest setting. Dust the sheets of dough as necessary to prevent sticking and cut the dough sheets to keep them at rectangles of manageable size as they pass through the finer settings of the machine.

Using a scalloped edged pastry cutter, trim each rectangular sheet of dough to make it even. Use the cutter to cut 7.5cm/3 inch-wide horizontal strips of dough. Roll the pastry cutter in the middle of the bottom, centre, and top of each strip taking care not to cut over the edges; the slashes will help the oil penetrate the inside of the dough, resulting in a well-puffed *galani*.

Heat the oil in a large flameproof pot to 180°C/350°F. Place just enough strips of dough into the hot oil to fit without crowding. Fry until golden and puffed, turning them once during cooking, 30 to 40 seconds per side. Transfer the *galani* to a kitchen paper-lined tray as they cook. To serve, mound the *galani* on a platter and dust with icing sugar.

Liguria

Liguria is set like a narrow
arch over the northern part
of the Mediterranean, spanning
270 kilometres from the
Pont St Louis on the French
frontier to the River Magra,
its border with Tuscany.

The Ligurians live between the sea and the mountains, which rise steeply a few kilometres inland, and in this narrow strip they have created one of the most luscious vegetable gardens in the whole of Europe. They have been helped by a steady temperate climate and the beneficial effect of the sea air on the plants, and the result is to be seen in the abundance of wild salads, aromatic herbs and succulent fruit and vegetables of almost every species.

It is the inhabitants, too, who are responsible for this abundance of produce; they are hard-working and parsimonious, a quality that has often been misunderstood in other parts of Italy as meanness. There is an amusing story of a Ligurian woman who goes to arrange the announcement of her husband's death. She tells the man to print 'Mario Rossi deceased.' 'Is that all?' says the man. 'Don't you want to say anything else? You can have three more words for the same price.' '*Ah, va bene, allora aggiunga "Fiat in vendita."*' Oh good, in that case add 'Fiat for sale'.

It is the fruits of their soil that have inspired the creativity of the local cooks. Meat and cereals were imported from Piedmont and Provence; on the peasant's table the only meat that appeared was rabbit. Still, now, if you go for a walk up the peaceful green hills that lie behind the overcrowded Riviera, you will see a row of rabbit hutches next to every house. Nearby there will be bushes of rosemary and sage growing strongly in the sun, and you can sense how this proximity will soon be sublimated in the kitchen. In Ventimiglia rabbits are stewed in local wine, with marjoram, sage, thyme and rosemary, enriched by the addition of local green olives.

Olive trees are abundant, and very productive on the Riviera di Ponente, the oil being delicate, sweet, pale in colour and of a taste which blends with every dish. The olive tree of Liguria is the Taggiasca variety, which produces small olives with very little pulp and a very high concentration of oil. These olives are the favourite of most Italian connoisseurs. The locals use them in their cooking as well, to flavour pot roasted rabbit, to layer with pancakes, to excite the flavour of fish and to enhance the local pizza. Olive oil is the only fat used in the local cooking: it dresses the many vegetable dishes for which the local cuisine is so well known.

Focaccia provides a good example of the qualities to be found in the local cuisine. It is simply bread dough, covered with sliced onions, stuffed with soft local cheese or sprinkled with olive pulp from the first pressing, and baked. Simple it may be, but in Liguria *focaccia* reaches perfection. This quality of 'just rightness' is achieved by finding the perfect balance between one flavour and another, and the precise use of ingredients. The end result is to transform a basically simple cuisine into a sophisticated demonstration of how to combine harmonizing elements. The supreme example of this is *pesto*, which is the most delightfully simple of all delicious sauces yet is only really delicious when made – by a Ligurian – with the local basil, and when the ingredients, pounded in a mortar, are just balanced correctly. Other examples of this perfect balance are found in the *preboggion*, a mixture of local herbs used for stuffing ravioli, and in all the stuffings for vegetables.

At noon, any town on the Riviera exudes a most appetizing smell. The pungent aroma of herbs mingles with the scent of charred courgettes, aubergines and fish, a combination that connects Genoa and all the coast to Middle Eastern, Arab and Spanish cooking. The influence of other Mediterranean countries is very strong, stronger in fact than it is in the cuisine of any other region. The local soft cheese, *prescinseua*, is very similar to Greek yogurt, *farinata* is a cousin of the Algerian *socca*, which reached Liguria via Nice, and in Savona there is a sort of soft bread which is very similar to pitta and which, like pitta, is used to contain other foods.

In Liguria even the puddings are based on local ingredients rather than imported ones. The spices that the Genoese carried to Europe on their ships seldom touched their food. When at home, they made use of fresh, locally grown fruits, and they learnt from the Arabs how to crystallize them. They became such experts that during the nineteenth century the European royal houses, Queen Victoria's among them, kept a purveyor of candied fruits in Genoa. Candied fruits, sultanas and pine nuts, all local products, appear in most of their sweets, from the *pan dolce*, a sort of *panettone* but less soft, to the delicate fried sweet ravioli.

OPPOSITE: *Olive flowers*

Cima Ripiena

Stuffed Breast of Veal

Ligurian food is often time-consuming to prepare, just like this dish. But the result – a plate of thin slices of tender succulent meat enriched with a very delicate stuffing – is well worth the trouble.

SERVES 8

1kg/2lb boned breast of veal
1 onion
1 celery stick
1 carrot
1 bay leaf
5 peppercorns, bruised
2 litres/3½ pints meat stock

FOR THE STUFFING
125g/4oz calf's sweetbread
50g/2oz day-old white bread, crusts
   removed
100ml/3½fl oz full-fat milk

juice of ½ lemon
1 small onion, finely chopped
25g/1oz unsalted butter
125g/4oz pie veal, fat removed, cut into
   very small pieces, or veal mince
25g/1oz pistachio nuts, blanched and peeled
2 tablespoons chopped fresh marjoram
1 egg, beaten
75g/3oz cooked peas
4 tablespoons freshly grated Parmesan
   cheese
salt and freshly ground black pepper

First prepare the stuffing. Wash the sweetbread under cold running water, then soak it in water for about 30 minutes. Meanwhile soak the bread in the milk for 15 minutes. Drain the sweetbread, put it into a saucepan of water with the lemon juice and a little salt, bring slowly to the boil and simmer for 15 minutes. Refresh the sweetbread under cold water and drain. Remove as much of the membranes and skin as you can and discard. Cut the sweetbread meat into small pieces.

Sauté the chopped onion in the butter for 3–4 minutes until golden. Add the veal and cook for 5 minutes, stirring frequently. Add the sweetbread and cook for a further 5 minutes. Add a little salt and pepper and remove from the heat. When cool, lift the meat out of the pan with a slotted spoon and chop finely (if using veal mince this is not necessary).

Scrape the onion and butter left in the pan into a bowl and mix together with the chopped meat, the pistachios, marjoram, beaten egg, peas, the bread with the milk squeezed out and the Parmesan. Taste and adjust the seasonings.

To stuff the veal, make a horizontal cut into the breast of the meat along the longer side, leaving the other sides uncut, like a pocket. Gently push the stuffing into this pocket, not too tightly because it will swell while cooking. Carefully sew up the opening and any holes you might have made while cutting the meat.

Meanwhile put the whole onion, celery, carrot, bay leaf and peppercorns into a large flameproof casserole or saucepan, cover with the stock and bring to the boil. When the stock is boiling, gently lower the stuffed meat into the casserole. Lower the heat and simmer for 1½ to 2 hours. When the time is up, allow to cool briefly and then lift the meat out of the pan and drain well. Transfer to a large roasting pan and place a heavy board on top. Weigh this down with heavy cans or weights. Leave in a cool place until completely cold. Cut into slices before serving.

Coniglio con Olive e Pinoli

Rabbit with Olives and Pine Nuts

The rabbit is one of the basic ingredients of rustic Ligurian cooking. It's prepared in a variety of ways, all using herbs and spices, as in this recipe from the Slow Food cookbook *Ricette di Osterie d'Italia*.

SERVES 6

extra virgin olive oil
1 garlic clove, finely chopped
½ onion, finely chopped
a bunch of fresh herbs (marjoram, thyme, rosemary and sage), finely chopped
a pinch of chilli powder

salt and freshly ground black pepper
110g/4oz Taggiasca olives
25g/1oz pine nuts
1 x 1.2kg/2½lb rabbit, cut into small pieces
500ml/18fl oz dry white wine

Pour a little olive oil into a large frying pan, add the garlic, onion, herbs, chilli powder, salt and pepper and cook gently until the onions are soft. Add the olives and pine nuts, then add the rabbit pieces and cook until the rabbit is browned on all sides. Pour over the wine and cook on a high heat for 5 minutes to let the alcohol evaporate. Cover the pan and cook on a low heat until the rabbit is tender and the sauce reduced.

CAMOGLI – LA SAGRA DEL PESCE

Camogli is one of the most beautiful places on earth – a claim that brings to mind what a little boy at a primary school in Sansepolcro in Tuscany said to his teacher when she told the class that Aldous Huxley described *The Resurrection* by Piero della Francesca as the most beautiful painting in the world. The boy asked, '*Mi scusi,* but has that English writer seen all the other paintings in the world?'

So, let me rephrase my opening sentence. Camogli is one of the most beautiful places I have ever seen. It is a town of tall, crooked houses painted in different hues of green, red, yellow and blue, all bunched together and looking out on to the Golfo Paradiso, the large gulf that extends from the northern side of the Portofino promontory to the city of Genoa. It is the picture postcard town par excellence. It is said that the houses are all painted in different colours so that sailors coming back from their long sea voyages would be able to recognize their houses from far away and point them out to their friends. Not only are they painted in different colours but they are embellished with *trompe-l'oeil* renditions of columns, garlands, capitals, statues, porticos and arches.

Camogli was a rich town up to the end of the nineteenth century. It was known as La Città dei Mille Velieri – the town of the thousand sailing boats, as it had very many boatbuilders. When propeller power began to replace sails, Camogli slowly began to lose its importance. But it still remains enchanting. In between the houses every little patch of land is bursting with greenery. When I was there last time, for La Sagra del Pesce, in May, the pittosporums were in full flower. The scent at night was overpowering and omnipresent, and it made me think with dismay of the pathetic, thin, sparse, scentless pittosporum in my garden in Dorset. Valerian was sprouting from every crack in every wall, tall and strong in its rich crimson or white colours.

La Sagra del Pesce is Camogli's biggest festival, and everybody was out enjoying themselves, thronging the steep narrow streets, the small harbour and the lovely promenade. Children were careering around with fish-shaped blue balloons in one hand and a *lecca-lecca* in the other. This festival is relatively modern: it was started in 1951 to give thanks to San Fortunato, the patron saint of fishermen, for his protection during the Second World War. The Camoglesi were very short of food, and at some point in the war the fishermen managed to go out for an entire night in a sea full of mines and come back safely with the most generous catch in years. The fish was layered in oil and brine, it was salted and air-dried, it was transformed into patés and sauces, and the Camoglesi managed to survive on that miraculous one-night catch.

The preparation for the *festa* starts a day or two in advance, when the 'sculpture' begins to be built on the beach. The sculpture is made of cardboard boxes, crates, papers, old chairs and other chattels, saved by the locals throughout the year. This year the sculpture was a magnificent dragon, about fifteen metres long, with a powerful green body and a proud red head.

On the Saturday evening there is the religious procession. The statue of San Fortunato is carried from the church, along the promenade and up the main streets for the locals to express their gratitude and pray. The statue, glittering with candles, is carried by six men, all in long white garments, followed by other similarly clad men with various headdresses, among them the occasional turban and fez. The women, dressed in black and holding the rosary, follow in prayer, and the band closes the procession, with throngs of children in tow. At first the band played solemn music, but towards the end the tempo changed. I suppose the players decided to cheer the people up, and they broke into a jolly tune. The carriers of the statue changed tempo too, and San Fortunato began to oscillate gaily from side to side, while one of the carriers was encouraging his partners with cries of 'San Fortunato olé!' I'm sure San Fortunato enjoyed this lively rhythm as much as we all did.

At 11.30 the fireworks started. They were all set on the beach and around the beautiful twelfth-century church perched on the rocks, straight over the sea. The church was lit up with flashes of red, green, blue and silver, and waterfalls of fire cascaded into the sea around it. A bonfire was lit under the dragon while a throng of firefighters, hose in hand, were making a watery barrier on the town side. The wind had come up quite strongly and the great crowd was standing back in awe.

The next day on the beach the dragon is a heap of ashes, a sad end for such a magnificent monster. At ten o'clock the parish priest walks down from his church to the little harbour to bless the fish, which is going to be fried and distributed to the people. On the quay a huge frying pan – four metres across in shining stainless steel – is ready. It is covered with a cheerful blue umbrella, which is there to channel the smoke into the six-metre-long handle that acts as a chimney.

In that majestic *padella* 1,000 litres of oil are bubbling, ready to receive the 3,000 tons of fish. The fish is all small blue fish – the poor man's fish. A posse of men and women, about thirty in number, are all around the *padella*, flouring the fish in large baskets. The baskets are lowered into the oil, go round the *padella* and come out *à point*. A sprinkling of salt, and the fish is placed in small plastic containers, to be handed out to the people who have queued patiently for this little, but meaningful, treat.

We were all very impressed by the smooth organization of the whole procedure. And sitting there in the sun, a glass of Vermentino in one hand and leisurely picking away at the little fried fish with the other, life was perfection.

Tellaro and the Octopus

Tellaro is one of the most beautiful villages at the south end of the Riviera di Levante – the eastern Riviera – and quite close to the border with Tuscany. It has a cluster of houses clinging to the slope of the hill all the way down to the small port, where the church rises as if from the sea.

There is a legend that says that on one stormy night the bells of the church suddenly began to ring. This was the alarm to the villagers to prepare for a raid by pirates. But on that night, when they got to the church they found that it was only a huge octopus playing with the bell ropes that reached down to the rocks.

This charming story was also quoted by D. H. Lawrence in 1913 in a letter to a friend. Lawrence had been captivated by the charm of Tellaro and used to spend quite a lot of time there.

OPPOSITE: *Fish for buridda*

Seppie in Umido con Patate e Piselli

Cuttlefish with Potatoes and Peas

There is a fish shop in the delightful town of Lerici, in the Gulf of the Poets where you can buy fresh fish as well as prepared fish dishes. A young and talented chef, Paolo, has given me the recipe for this excellent one-pot dish.

SERVES 4

1kg/2lb cuttlefish
5 tablespoons extra virgin olive oil
1 small onion, chopped
a dozen fresh basil leaves, torn into pieces
1 or 2 small dried chillies
salt and feshly ground black pepper

300ml/½ pint dry white wine
4 ripe fresh tomatoes, peeled
500g/1lb waxy potaotes, peeled and cut into
*   chunks*
350g/1½oz fresh peas, podded or
*   frozen peas*

Have the cuttlefish cleaned by the fishmonger. When you are at home, cut the tentacles and the sacs into pieces.

Heat the oil and sauté the onion until just soft. Throw in the basil, chilli and salt and pepper. Sauté for a couple of minutes and then add the fish and cook for about 5 minutes, turning it over and over. Splash with the wine and let it evaporate. Now add the tomatoes and continue cooking for a further 5 minutes before you add the potatoes. Turn the heat down and keep a watch over the pan. You might have to add a little water every now and then if the dish gets too dry.

If you are using fresh peas, add tham about 7-10 minutes after you have added the potatoes. If you are using frozen peas, add them when the potatoes are cooked, as they only need a few minutes. Taste and check the seasoning before you bring the dish to the table.

FRANCE v. ITALY –
A GASTRONOMIC WAR

The French and the Italians have for ever been at war on matters gastronomic, which seems to me a highly civilized way to be at war. Quite a few dishes have dual nationality, but where they really originated is not 100 per cent certain. We find these dishes in Liguria, Piedmont and Lombardy, regions that have been influenced by, and have in their turn influenced the cooking of France.

Is pesto a Ligurian invention, or an Italianization of the Provençal *pistou*? Did *pissaladière* derive from *pissaladeira*, or the other way round? What about *bourride* and *buridda*, the fish soups of Nice and the western Riviera? And finally what about *marrons glacés*? I'm partial, of course. Of these four dishes, the only one for which even I cannot claim solely Italian origins is *buridda*, a soup made with an assortment of fish and seafood. In the past it was the soup of the poor, made wherever there was a fish market, with the fish that remained unsold at the end of the morning. The fish of the French and Italian Rivieras are similar; add oil, garlic and tomatoes and the result is similar too, the only difference being that *bourride* is often served with aïoli.

Pesto is Ligurian because it is in Liguria, and not in Provence, that the best basil grows. The French, in their *pistou*, have eliminated the cheese and the pine nuts. That said, it seems to me that both mixtures are so intrinsic to the local food that they are a natural local creation. *Pissaladière* and *pissaladeira*, also called *sardenaria*, is a more complex dish. It consists of a pizza covered with onions, black olives and preserved anchovies. Nowadays some cooks add tomatoes to the Italian version, which I find objectionable, as the dish existed at least two centuries before tomatoes became popular in Italy. The name *pissaladeira* is a dialectization of *pizza all'Andrea*, the favourite pizza of the great admiral of the Genoese Republic – Andrea Doria. From Sanremo, where some gastronomic historians say it originates, it was a step for it to reach the border and become Niçoise.

And finally *marrons glacés*, which, it has been established, are definitely of Ligurian origin in spite of their French name. They were created on the western Riviera, probably in Savona, and during the French occupation of Genoa in the eighteenth century they were brought to France where they were christened *marrons glacés*, a lovely name that gave them the right credentials at a time when France was the gastronomic leader.

BASIL

No other herb, vegetable or flower is more emblematic of Liguria than basil. It flourishes everywhere, in pots on windowsills, in gardens and in large plantations in the fields. Basil is noble in its name, which comes from *basilikos*, meaning king in Greek. 'In antiquity it was considered indeed a sacred plant which should be cut only with an instrument of noble metal by a person who had previously performed purificatory rites.' Thus wrote Waverley Root in his book *The Food of Italy*. To this day it is said that basil should be torn or pounded rather than chopped with a knife, supposedly because the metal might affect the flavour, although surely the notion also stems from superstition. Why should this be the only herb affected by metal?

Basil is surrounded by legends and stories. In one of Boccaccio's stories basil becomes the symbol of love when the fair and noble Lisabetta, whose brothers have murdered her plebeian lover, buries that lover's head in a pot of basil. Keats takes up the story in his poem *Isabella; or The Pot of Basil*, from which these are brief and poignant extracts:

> She wrapped it up; and for its tomb did choose
> A garden-pot, wherein she laid it by,
> And covered it with mould, and o'er it set
> Sweet basil, which her tears kept ever wet...
>
> And so she ever fed it with thin tears,
> Whence thick, and green, and beautiful it grew,
> So that it smelt more balmy than its peers
> Of basil-tufts in Florence...
>
> And so she pined, and so she died forlorn,
> Imploring for her basil to the last...

By way of complete contrast, John Raymond, writing in 1648 about his travels in Italy, reports: 'Amongst their Medicinall Plants scarce knowne amongst us but in Apothicaries shoppes; I took notice of one Odiferous Hearbe called Basilico, which hath this innate power, that if laid under a stone in some moyst place, in two dayes it produceth a Scorpion, this I can assert by experience, and to countenance this story, there fell out a strange accident in my stay in Siena. A gentleman was so pleased with the smell of this Basilico, that he had some dry'd and beaten into powder, which he snuft up, imagining it of the same force with Tobacco to cleare the head, but hee bought the experience at the price of his life, for hee dyed distracted; his skull being afterwards opened by the Chyrurgion, a nest of Scorpions were found feeding on his Braine.'

Basil, which came originally from India, established itself very well in Italy and especially in Liguria, the region that popularized it with the well-known sauce pesto. It is said that basil grows so well in Liguria thanks to the humid breezes from the sea and the hot sun. But Liguria, a very thin strip of territory skirting a large arc of the Mediterranean, is steeply mountainous and the land has to be terraced in order that it can be cultivated. As a result there isn't enough basil in Liguria to satisfy all the people worldwide yearning for their pots of pesto. So now basil is also grown in southern Piedmont, just the other side of the Appennines, with Ligurian sea breezes blowing north through the valleys to give the necessary breath of salty air to the fields.

Minestrone alla Genovese
Minestrone with Crushed Garlic

Minestrone is often served with a spoonful of the Ligurian favourite pesto sauce, as in this recipe. If you don't have time to make a pesto, you can always buy a jar of ready-made pesto instead.

SERVES 4–6

3 small aubergines, roughly chopped
150g/5oz green beans, cut into short lengths
*150g/5oz fresh **borlotti** beans, cooked in*
    boiling water until tender
3 or 4 potatoes, peeled and chopped
½ cabbage, sliced
a small piece of pumpkin, diced
3 or 4 tomatoes, roughly chopped
75g/3oz fresh mushrooms

olive oil
a handful of tagliatelle or other pasta
FOR THE PESTO
1 garlic clove
a small bunch of basil
*a handful of **pecorino sardo** cheese, grated*
*a handful of **Parmesan** cheese, grated*
    plus extra to serve
a knob of unsalted butter

Bring a large pan of salted water to the boil. Add the aubergines, green beans and borlotti beans. Leave to simmer for 10 minutes, then add the potatoes, cabbage, pumpkin, tomatoes, mushrooms and 2 tablespoons of olive oil. Simmer until the vegetables are almost tender. Add the pasta to the pan and continue cooking until al dente.

Make a pesto by crushing the garlic clove together with the basil, *pecorino sardo* and Parmesan. Melt the butter in a small pan with a little olive oil and a dash of warm water, add the pesto and cook gently until softened. Serve the soup with the pesto spooned on top and with more grated Parmesan.

OVERLEAF: *Ingredients for pesto*

PESTO

'And what is this scent of alpine herbs that mixes so strangely with the smell of the rocks, pervading the air of all the Riviera from Lerici to Turbia? All the region is enveloped by it as from the surf of the sea. It is a lively and exciting scent. It is the scent of pesto, the condiment made with basil, pecorino, garlic, pine nuts, beaten in a mortar and diluted with olive oil. Is that all? Yes, that is all, and a unique thing is created. There are condiments that appear in many regions, but this is solely Ligurian, it speaks the Ligurian dialect.' Thus wrote Paolo Monelli in his best seller *Il Ghiottone Errante* (The Wandering Gourmand), a gastronomic tour of Italy published in 1935.

To this day pesto to any Italian means Liguria. It is strange to think that until about twenty years ago it was hardly known outside the region. I was lucky enough to enjoy pesto even as a child, in spite of not living there – we used to spend our long summer holidays in Liguria, by the sea, and my mother would make jars of pesto to bring back to Milan, but when it was finished, that was that. It was one of the many joys of going to Liguria, along with eating ripe figs straight from the tree, soft and warm from the sun. At the time, and even much later, I did wonder why this green ambrosia had never travelled beyond the boundaries of its birthplace and invaded at least the nearby regions. And then, about ten years ago, the explosion started, so that now, from Japan to Peru, pesto is scooped out of glass jars and enjoyed.

Pesto is made differently in each part of Liguria, and in the hands of different cooks. Fundamentally, however, there are two basic recipes. The pesto of the western Riviera and of Genoa contains more garlic, being similar to the Provençal *pistou*. It is a coarser and more energetic pesto than that of the eastern Riviera, which is more delicate thanks to the addition of *prescinseua* – a sort of curd cheese – or even butter. My mother, who was a great cook, added a lump of soft butter to her pesto, as does Marcella Hazan, in order to *aggraziarlo* – make it more graceful.

The American writer Fred Plotkin, in his book *Recipes from Paradise*, which in my opinion is the best account of Ligurian food and cooking, gives fifteen recipes for pesto from different places, ending with a recipe for blender pesto. Quite rightly he points to the inferiority of this recipe compared to pesto made in a mortar. He writes, 'The difference is because the flavours of the ingredients are released more slowly and gently in the mortar.' And that is very true. Having said that, however, I feel quite happy, when I am short of time, to use a food processor, time being now the scarcer ingredient in any recipe.

Some years ago I went to see the fields of basil grown by the Amadeis brothers in southern Piedmont. On the long trestle table under the majestic walnut tree there were bowls of different pestos for us to taste. I asked Carla Amadeis how often she made it. 'Oh, very rarely,' she answered. 'I usually use Sacla' Organic Pesto.' Well, if Sacla' pesto is good enough for a basil grower, I feel it is good enough for us all.

Pesto della Riviera di Levante

Pesto of the eastern Riviera

I have chosen the recipe for this pesto because it is the one most commonly used these days. Choose a mild extra virgin olive oil, not a peppery one, so as not to upset the balance of flavours. When you can't find a good basil or when you are short of time, do what Carla Amadeis, the basil grower does: use a jar of ready-made pesto instead.

FOR 4 PORTIONS OF PASTA

25g/1oz pine nuts
60g/2½oz fresh basil leaves
1 garlic clove
a pinch of coarse sea salt
4 tablespoons freshly grated
  Parmesan cheese

2 tablespoons freshly grated mature
  pecorino cheese
125ml/4fl oz extra virgin olive oil,
  preferably Ligurian

Heat the oven to 180°C/350°F/Gas Mark 4. Spread the pine nuts on a baking tray and put the tray into the oven for 3 to 4 minutes.

Put the basil leaves, garlic clove, pine nuts and salt into a mortar and grind against the sides of the mortar with a pestle, crushing all the ingredients, until the mixture has become a rough paste. Mix in the grated cheeses and pour over the oil very gradually, beating with a wooden spoon. If you want to make your pesto in a food processor or a blender, put all the ingredients in the bowl and whizz until finely chopped. Stop every now and then and scrape down the pesto with a spatula. When the mixture is evenly blended, add the cheeses and whizz for a second or two.

Pesto freezes very well. Freeze in sealed jars, without adding the Parmesan and pecorino. Thaw overnight, and when completely thawed mix in the cheeses.

PASTA

Although pasta does not have its origins in Liguria, its first documentation comes in fact from there. It is a 1244 contract written in Genoa, which mentions *pasta liscia ossia secca* – dried pasta. A few years later, in 1279, a *baricella piena* – a basketful – *di macaronis* appears in the list of items left on his death by one Ponzio Bastone. The mention of the basket is interesting for two reasons: first, because it is one of the earliest known references to dried pasta, and second, because since it was listed separately by the notary, macaroni must have been something of a luxury, rather than an ordinary food.

But certainly Liguria is the motherland of ravioli (the name allegedly coming from the surname of an innkeeper – Raviolo), which is now the name given worldwide to most shapes of stuffed pasta. In Liguria they are filled with meat, fish or vegetables, as in other regions. But the stuffed pasta shapes that are exclusively Ligurian are the *pansôti*, which are *cappelletti*-like shapes but much fatter, as their name implies, *pansôti* meaning 'with a large belly'. While *cappelletti* are filled with half a teaspoon of stuffing, *pansôti* need a whole teaspoon. *Pansôti* are filled with *preboggion*, a mixture of the wild herbs that grow on the sunny Ligurian hills: borage, beets, sorrel, dandelion, chervil, wild chicory or an assortment of all of these. The traditional dressing is walnut sauce.

The other local pasta is *corzetti*, of which there are two kinds, *corzetti dei Fieschi* and *corzetti della Valpolcevera*. The first are stamped discs of pasta. The stamps are handmade in wood and imitate a coin of the Republic of Genoa, with different old designs, among which those of the coats-of-arms of the two most powerful Genoese families, the Fieschi and the Doria, are the most common. The pasta dough is stretched out not too thin and then stamped. The little cooked discs can be dressed with a delicate marjoram and pine nut pesto or with the more common basil pesto. The most famous are the *corzetti dei Fieschi* made in the town of Recco on the eastern Riviera. The *corzetti alla Valpolcevera* originate from the *entroterra* – the hinterland – of Genoa. They are small, shaped like a figure eight, and are usually served with a *tocco di funghi* – mushroom sauce, the other great Ligurian sauce.

Other typical Ligurian shapes are *trenette*, *trofie*, *picagge* and *mandili de saea*. *Trenette*, like wide *linguine*, and *trofie*, like small corkscrews, are traditionally served with pesto. *Picagge* – ribbons in Genoese dialect – are wide tagliatelle about six centimetres in width and are usually dressed with meat juices, but not a *ragù*, and plenty of Parmesan. *Mandili de saea* (*saea* is dialect for *seta*, silk) is the poetic name for the common lasagne, rolled out as thinly as possible, just like silk, usually dressed with pesto or with *tocco di funghi*.

Tocco di Noci

Walnut Sauce

Fred Plotkin writes in his excellent book *Recipes from Paradise* that *tocco di noci* is the traditional dressing for *pansôti*, the herb-filled pasta of Liguria. 'But,' he continues, 'the walnut sauce is also very good with gnocchi, tortelloni or even with boiled meats such as pork or veal.' And I couldn't agree more, adding poached chicken to the list. Here is his recipe.

MAKES ABOUT 225ML/7FL OZ

200g/7oz fresh or shelled walnuts
25g/1oz unflavoured breadcrumbs
1 garlic clove, minced
30g/1oz finely grated Parmesan cheese
1 pinch of minced fresh marjoram

175ml/6fl oz **prescinseua** *(Ligurian curd cheese) or 150g/5fl oz fresh ricotta diluted with 2 tablespoons tepid water*
60ml/2½fl oz extra virgin olive oil, preferably Ligurian, plus extra to taste
sea salt (optional)

Place the walnuts, breadcrumbs, garlic and salt in a mortar and pound with a pestle to form a paste. Alternatively place these ingredients in a blender or food processor and blend until they form a paste. Transfer to a bowl if you are not using a pestle and mortar. Add the Parmesan and marjoram, then the *prescinseua* or diluted ricotta. Finally, add the olive oil to the mixture, a little at a time, stirring to combine the ingredients. Serve on hot pasta.

VEGETABLE PIES,
TARTS AND FOCACCE

Thanks to its sheltered climate, hot sun and sea breezes, Liguria has some of the most fertile vegetable gardens in Italy. The production is small, but what is produced is of the best. The purple asparagus and the artichokes of Albenga, the garlic of Vessalico and the beans of Badalucco are among the most highly regarded vegetables in Italy. Not only are the Ligurians expert at producing the best vegetables, they also know the best ways to cook them and have created an array of outstanding vegetable dishes. Ligurian cooking is a '*cucina povera*', the best dishes being based on what used to be 'poor' ingredients such as vegetables, rabbit and fish.

Vegetables are used in a most skilful way to create delicious dishes in their own right. Of these, the *torta pasqualina* is emblematic of the region. It is a pie of thirty-three layers of a pastry similar to filo, enveloping sliced baby artichokes, hard-boiled eggs and soft cheese. The thirty-three layers represent the years of the life of Christ, and the pie is ritually eaten on Easter Sunday. *Torta pasqualina* is filled with spinach, Swiss chard or courgettes when artichokes are not in season. Other pies contain rice as well as a vegetable. The Ligurian *polpettoni* are similar vegetable dishes, but without crusts. *Polpettone* of French beans and potatoes and *polpettone* of courgettes are the most popular.

The Ligurians also excel in the art of stuffing, which developed from the need to make an ingredient go further with the help of breadcrumbs, eggs, ricotta and other cheap foods. There are endless versions of stuffed vegetables, the most common being courgettes, round aubergines, onions and lettuces. Cheap cuts of meat, such as breast of veal, are stuffed, as are sardines and cuttlefish. Porcini caps, from porcini gathered on the Apennines, are also stuffed, while the very popular *tocco di funghi* mushroom sauce, used to dress pasta, is made with all sorts of mushrooms plus a small handful of dried *porcini*. The composer Rossini, a famous gourmet and connoisseur of excellent food, had dried Ligurian *porcini* sent to him while he was living in Paris.

In no other region is there such an assortment of *focacce* as in Liguria, and in no other region is *focaccia* so good. *Focaccia* is basically bread dough to which olive oil, and sometimes other ingredients, are added. It might be because of the olive oil, the black Taggiasca olives, the white onions, the soft local cheese, the scented rosemary or the skill of the baker, but a *focaccia* eaten straight out of the oven while walking by the Ligurian seaside is the best food in the world. Maybe it is even better than a slice of *farinata*, cut from the huge circle baked in a copper pan just out of the oven, wrapped in absorbent brown paper and dripping oil down your chin. *Farinata* is a paper-thin chickpea tart, and it is the autumn alternative to the all-year-round *focaccia*.

There is a charming story about *focaccia* with onion in Fred Plotkin's splendid book *Recipes from Paradise*. Plotkin, who lives part of the time in Camogli, writes, 'The women of Camogli have told me that in the past it was the custom for women to eat onion *focaccia* just before their men went to sea. As the sailors and fishermen were set to embark, their wives and girl friends would give them a big onion-scented kiss that would supposedly make the men less desirable to women in other ports.'

Capponadda

Vegetable and Fish Salad

The Ristorante Rosa is situated up the hill above Camogli, and its view of the whole of the Golfo Paradiso is indeed superb. Signora Costa, the owner, gave us the recipe for her excellent capponadda, a local dish which has its origins in the time when sailors from Camogli used to sail all over the Mediterranean in their splendid sailing boats.

Capponadda should contain *mosciame* – dried tuna, very thinly cut.

SERVES 8

6 Genovese **gallette** *(crackers)*
1 garlic clove, cut in half
2 tablespoons balsamic vinegar
4 tomatoes, ripe but firm, cut into segments
12 salted anchovies, cleaned
300g/10oz tuna preserved in oil, flaked
150g/5oz stoned black olives
25g/1oz capers

150g/5oz Italian onions, pickled in
  balsamic vinegar
1 tablespoon extra virgin olive oil
6 hard-boiled eggs
16 slices of **mosciame** *(dried tuna),*
  if available
8–12 red peppers preserved in oil
chopped fresh oregano

Rub the *gallette* with the cut sides of the garlic and put them into a bowl with a little water and vinegar. Leave to get soft.

Break the *gallette* up and put them back into the bowl. Add the tomatoes, anchovies, tuna, olives, capers and onions. Dress with olive oil and vinegar and mix well. Spoon the mixture on to a serving dish. Decorate with the hard-boiled eggs, cut into segments, the *mosciame* and the peppers and sprinkle with oregano.

Zucchine Ripiene

Stuffed Courgettes

An excellent recipe by Fred Plotkin from his book *Recipes from Paardise*.

SERVES 2 AS A MAIN COURSE OR 4 AS AN ANTIPASTO

4 medium courgettes, or preferably
  8 baby courgettes
1 tablespoon/7g unsalted butter
3 tablespoons/20g finely chopped onion
150g/5oz ground veal or lean beef
35g/1½oz **prosciutto crudo,** *minced*
2 large eggs, lightly beaten
35g/1½oz unseasoned breadcrumbs

60g/2½oz freshly grated Parmesan
freshly ground black pepper
fine sea salt
a few fresh basil leaves, carefully wiped
  and torn into small bits
350ml/12fl oz tomato sauce or purée
Ligurian extra virgin olive oil

Preheat the oven to 180°C/350°F/Gas Mark 4. Set a large pot of cold water to boil. When it reaches a boil, add the courgettes and cook for 5 minutes. Remove them from the pot, let cool for a couple of minutes and then slice them in half lengthwise. Carefully scoop out the pulp, making sure not to break the shell of the courgettes. Place the pulp in a large mixing bowl.

Melt the butter in a frying pan. Add the onion and sauté for a few seconds. Then add the veal or beef and cook gently for 1 minute, pushing the meat around in the pan so that it cooks evenly and does not stick. Then add the *prosciutto* and continue cooking until the meat is thoroughly browned.

Drain all the cooking fat and then add the meat and onion mixture to the courgette pulp. Add the eggs, breadcrumbs, Parmesan, pepper, salt and basil leaves to the bowl and combine with a wooden spoon. Once the mixture is well-blended, spoon it into the 8 courgette halves. Pour the tomato sauce into a large baking dish that has been lightly greased with olive oil. Carefully place the courgettes into the dish and bake for 15 to 20 minutes, or until the filling is browned but not overdone. Serve hot, warm or at room temperature with a bit of tomato sauce from the dish.

OVERLEAF: *Blue asparagus of Liguria*

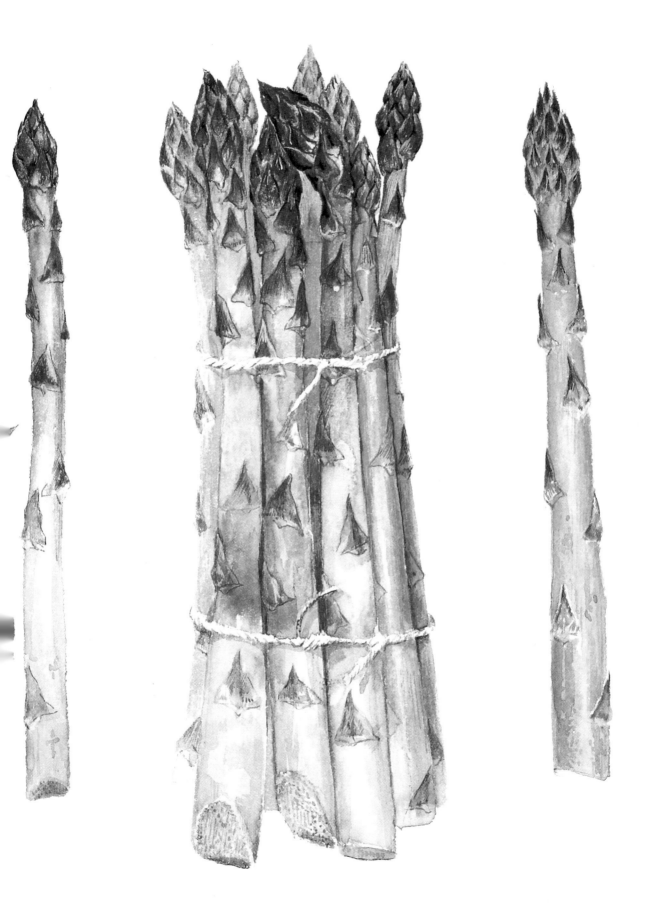

Torta Pasqualina

Savoury Easter Pie

SERVES 6

FOR THE DOUGH
315g/11oz flour
2 tablespoons extra virgin olive oil

FOR THE STUFFING
olive oil
1 large onion, chopped

2 garlic cloves, chopped
1 sprig of fresh parsley, chopped
1 kg chard, chopped, or 10 globe
*   artichokes, prepared and sliced*
3 bunches of fresh borage, chopped
8 eggs
salt and freshly ground black pepper

Preheat the oven to 200°C/400°F/Gas Mark 6. Put the flour into a large bowl or on to a work surface. Make a well in the middle and add a pinch of salt and the olive oil. Knead well, gradually adding water, until the dough becomes elastic. Knead for 10 minutes, then divide the dough into 6 pieces and put them on a baking tray. Cover them with a damp teatowel and set aside for 1 hour.

Heat a little olive oil in a frying pan and add the onion, garlic and parsley. Cook for a few minutes, until the onion is soft, then add the chard or artichokes and the borage and cook for a further 15 minutes. Allow to cool. Beat 3 of the eggs, season with salt and pepper, and mix with the cooked vegetables. Set aside.

Grease a 30cm/12 inch round cake tin. Roll out each piece of dough on a floured board into a circle about 1cm/½ inch larger than your tin. Place the first circle of dough in the tin and brush the surface with oil. Place another circle of dough over it and then a third. Spread the vegetable mixture over the dough and make 5 small depressions in it, close to the edge. Break a raw egg into each of these and sprinkle with salt, pepper and oil. Cover with the remaining circles of dough, each brushed with oil. Pinch the edges and trim off the excess dough, then prick the top of the pie in a few places and brush with oil.

Bake in the preheated oven for about 1 hour, then remove from the oven and serve at room temperature.

CANDITI E SCIROPPI

Genoa and the western Riviera have for centuries been the producers of the best candied fruits and flower syrups. The basic reason for this is the climate of the area, where all sorts of fruits flourish and where flowers have traditionally been raised in the nurseries in the valleys behind Sanremo and Bordighera. As a result the drawing rooms of the wealthy northerners could always be 'in bloom' and their tables could be enriched and embellished with delicious candied fruits.

Of all the fruits that grow on the western Riviera, one is unique to that area: the *chinotto*. The *chinotto* is a fruit of the same species as the Seville orange, brought from China (as the name makes clear) at the beginning of the sixteenth century. It is a small greenish fruit of intense fragrance, never eaten raw because it is too bitter, but excellent when candied or preserved in sugar syrup. Before the war most bars in northern Italy had on the counter a large jar full of *chinotti* in syrup. You pushed a long two-pronged fork in and popped a round green ball into your mouth, which at the first bite was filled with a heavenly citrus flavour. After the war *chinotti* disappeared, but now, thanks to Slow Food, they are coming back.

They are grown near the town of Savona on the western Riviera and soon, I hope, they will take their place on the counters of the best bars.

The first *chinotti* were candied by the French in the eighteenth century, and it is indeed from the French that the Ligurians learnt the craft of making candied fruits. There is one exception, the *marron glacé*, which, in spite of its name, was first produced in Savona and then taken over by the French and re-christened. By the end of the eighteenth century the candied fruits produced in Liguria were competing with French ones, and the best patisseries of Genoa took their cue from those in Paris, soon to become the leaders. Of these, the Confetteria Romanengo was, and still is, the best known. In the nineteenth century it exported candied fruits to all the royal houses of Europe and indeed to the whole world.

Another area of produce in Liguria, akin to the candied fruits, is that of rose syrup, candied rose petals and rose preserves, all of which the Genoese must have learnt to make from the Arabs. These are all made from the petals of old types of rose, such as Gallicas and Rugosas. These roses are cultivated in a valley behind Genoa, which in May seems to explode with deep crimson, deeply fragrant flowers. The nineteenth-century recipe for the syrup is very simple: just rose petals, water, sugar and some lemon juice to bring out the aroma. This recipe is still used today. In the past the syrup was served hot in the winter, like a punch, and cold in the summer.

There are only a few producers of this exquisite old-fashioned product, but Slow Food, which has created a Presidium to protect it, is rightly trying to make rose syrup better known.

Sciumette

Soft Meringues in Custard

Sciumette are the Genovese version of the French *isles flottantes*. This recipe was given to me by Cristina Carboni, the owner of the restaurant Manuelina in Recco, best known for its *focaccia al formaggio*.

SERVES 4

4 eggs, separated
75g/3oz caster sugar
1 litre/1½ pints full-fat milk

1 tablespoon flour
powdered cinnamon

Whisk the egg whites with 25g/1oz of the sugar. Bring the milk to the boil, then drop the egg and sugar mixture by spoonfuls into it. Let each blob become solid, then lift them out with a slotted spoon and drain.

Remove the milk from the heat and add the remaining sugar and 1 tablespoon of flour. Mix well and allow the mixture to cool. Beat the egg yolks and fold into the milk mixture. Return the custard to the heat and heat until very hot, but not boiling.

To serve, spoon a layer of custard on to each plate, place a *sciumetta* on top, and sprinkle with cinnamon.

OVERLEAF: *Candied fruit from Romanengo in Genoa*

Le Marche

Le Marche is a region whose hilltop towns speak of its history. The tall and powerful pink palaces point directly to the Stato Pontificio – Vatican state – of which for centuries Le Marche was a part.

OPVS · CAROLI · CRIVELLI · VENETI

The Marchigiani, both patricians and plebs, gave the Catholic Church many priests, monseigneurs and cardinals. Le Marche can also boast great artists, such as Raphael, politicians and military men, among them Federico da Montefeltro Duca d'Urbino, poets, such as Giacomo Leopardi, and musicians, such as Gioacchino Rossini. The region has a majestic serenity that envelopes and entrances. Life has a slower tempo there, and when you arrive you feel you step back fifty years in time.

This pleasant aura of the everyday life of days gone by also pervades the cooking, still unspoilt by modern whims of international fantasy, still based on the produce of the sea, the hills and the mountains. The long and flat coast makes up for its tedious sameness by offering a variety of fish unequalled in other regions. It includes crustaceans, from the aristocratic spiny lobsters and langoustines to the plebeian *cannocchie* (mantis shrimp); octopus, cuttlefish and squid; mussels and clams; sardines and mackerel in their blue-green livery; and an array of sole, hake, monkfish, rascasse – all of which finish up in the pot to make the local *brodetto* – fish soup.

The cooking of the hills reflects the richness of the land, with dishes of vegetables, chicken, rabbit and pork, while further up the Apennines the food becomes rough and sturdy, with lamb, pulses and fungi. But of all meat it is the pig that reigns supreme. It appears in its most popular form as *porchetta*, on stalls on market days and at village feasts, rich with garlic and herbs, to be enjoyed just on the spot with chunks of local bread, coarse and thick and unsalted, the perfect accompaniment to the sapidity of the meat.

Porchetta is indeed the festive dish of the region, but wild boar is grander and more stylish. It is the meat to be served on special occasions, as it was indeed served at the Agriturismo Villa Cicchi, near Ascoli Piceno, at a christening party. The wild boar came from the large farm of the Cicchi nearby, where the animals roam freely as in the wild. It had been marinated for twenty-four hours in a *battuto* (chopped mixture) of rosemary, wild fennel, grated lemon zest and garlic. It was then placed on a wire rack over a pan and red wine was poured over the beast just before it was put into the hot bread oven. The cooking juices collected in the pan were used to douse the boar during the cooking. Some three and a half hours later the glistening boar was transferred to a wooden platter decorated with branches of variegated ivy and bay leaf and paraded round the tables to the applause of the diners, before being carved to even greater applause.

I am sorry to say that I didn't have even the smallest mouthful of the beast. The boar made its glorious appearance at half past three, by which time I had even had my *espresso*. But I can testify to the excellent cooking of the Villa Cicchi, where all the ingredients are made with their own produce. My *fritto marchigiano* was delicious. Like *porchetta*, the *fritto marchigiano* is also a festive dish, combining vegetables, meat and even sweet things all on the same plate. The meat at the Villa Cicchi was lamb chops, so tiny that the lamb couldn't have been older than two or three months, courgettes, onions, peppers, *olive ascolane*, sage leaves and crème patissière. The crème patissière is what makes this *fritto* so special. The cold custard is cut into little squares which are coated in flour, egg and breadcrumbs and fried in plenty of Ascolano olive oil, as are all the other ingredients. The creator of this masterpiece was Elena Cicchi, who, with her mother and sister, runs the Agriturismo, while her husband and her brother-in-law are the *rôtissiers*. Having seen the wild boar, I felt Brillat-Savarin could have been referring to them when he wrote, '*On devient cuisinier, mais on nait rôtissier*' – one becomes a cook but one is born a *rôtissier*.

Further up the Apennines, black and white truffles can be found, so good as to compete with the famous *tartufi neri* of Norcia in Umbria and the *tartufi bianchi* of Alba in Piedmont. In fact the locals told me that the white truffles of Acqualagna in northern Marche are sent to Alba to be sold as the more famous *tartufi d'Alba*. The woods are rich with fungi of many varieties, from the princely *porcini* and *ovuli* to the more modest wood blewit, parasol and *Lactarius deliciosus*.

Apples from Monti Sibillini

Olive groves are everywhere, especially around the stunningly beautiful Ascoli Piceno, which the French writer André Gide described as *'la plus belle ville d'Italie'*. The olive trees there are of the Ascolana Tenera variety, which are grown only around Ascoli and with which the stuffed *olive ascolane* are made, the most famous dish of the region.

In northern Marche, near Urbino, another Marchigiano jewel, an extraordinary pecorino is made: the *pecorino di fosse*. These *fosse* are caves of tufa in which the cheeses are aged. The cheeses stay there from two to six months, as do most *pecorini*. But here in the tufa caves, the cheese absorbs the smell of the tufa. It sounds unpleasant but I can assure you that it is sublime, especially as it was served at the restaurant of the Fortino Napoleonico hotel in Portonovo, surrounded by a golden pool of acacia honey.

But never mind about olives, *pecorini* and wild boars, to me the symbol of Le Marche is the fruit. The wide valleys of the rivers that flow from the Apennines down to the Adriatic are filled with orchards: pears, cherries, apricots, apples, walnuts and peaches, especially the juicy white and yellow peaches and the squashed variety called Saturnia, which has the most intense flavour and which is now being cultivated again after years of neglect. The nectarines I ate there reminded me of this description by John Keats in a letter to Charles Dilke: 'Talking of Pleasure, this moment I was writing with one hand and with the other holding to my mouth a nectarine – good god, how fine! It went down soft and pulpy, slushy, oozy – all its delicious embonpoint melted down my throat like a large beautiful strawberry.' I wonder if the nectarine came from Le Marche. Figs, I was told, are also being brought back into cultivation, after having been felled during the '60s and '70s to make room for more industrialized crops.

The other great produce of the region is the cucurbit family, in all its range and variety: huge watermelons, so invitingly cool on a summer afternoon, yellow melons to crown a dish of *prosciutto*, jade green cucumbers to be sliced into a salad – all ready to be eaten or indeed painted, as they were by Carlo Crivelli. Crivelli, a fifteenth-century Venetian, spent most of his life in Le Marche. He must have enjoyed the sight of all those beautiful peaches and melons and pomegranates and cucumbers so much that he festooned his madonnas and his saints with garlands of them. Crivelli's baby Jesuses must have feasted on them.

L'ANTICA CUCINA POVERA DELLE MARCHE

THE PEASANT COOKING OF LE MARCHE

Le Marche is a region that has kept its old traditions longer than most other parts of Italy. This is probably due to its late industrialization and the slow pace of life. It is also one of the regions where the cooking varies incredibly, even within a distance of a few miles. When I was there I was lucky enough to come across quite a few people who helped me a lot with my research. One was Peppa (see page 164) and another was Giovanni Giustozzi, who owns and cooks at the Ristorante Pizzeria La Torre in Monteleone di Fermo, where the food is excellent and the view is spectacular. With that view of the Marchigiane hills dotted with olive trees, walnut trees, fields of sunflowers and wheat, like a padded patchwork, you can enjoy the array of dishes that keeps on being set in front of you. The *antipasti* always include the two classics, *stoccafisso e patate* – stockfish and potatoes – and *calamari fritti*. *Stoccafisso e patate* used to be the dish of the *contadini*, who enjoyed having it brought to them in the fields to eat at midday; now it is the dish of the '*signori*' because of the price of the fish. The stockfish is soaked for at least four long days before being added, cut in chunks, to the potatoes stewed in tomato sauce.

Two other old peasant dishes served at La Torre are sausages with eggs (see page 146), which is similar to *coradella* with eggs – lamb offal finished off with eggs and lemon juice, and a juicy and tender dish of tripe floating in a rich and piquant tomato sauce. All offal is treated with great respect and imagination, as are vegetables and pulses, which become excellent dishes in their own right.

In Urbino, at the Trattoria del Leone, I came across my favourite peasant dish. It was a yellow mountain of tagliatelle dressed, simply, with breadcrumbs, oil and garlic. The breadcrumbs, from finely crumbled white bread, are sautéd with a lovely bunch of parsley in a good deal of oil flavoured with chopped garlic. In about five or six minutes they are ready to receive the drained tagliatelle. Another *cucina povera* pasta dish I had never had before was *passatelli* with a vegetable *ragù*. *Passatelli* are a kind of short thick pasta made at home, with breadcrumbs, eggs and Parmesan. I knew the *passatelli* of Romagna, the region to the north of Le Marche,

rich in Parmesan and floating in clear meat stock, but here in Urbino they were drained and dressed with a vegetable mixture. I was told that the difference between the two is that those of Le Marche contain less cheese because this region is poorer than Romagna, but that there is plenty of good bread and plenty of excellent vegetables to dress them.

Of all meat, it used to be the rabbit that appeared most regularly on Marchigiane tables. Every family had a rabbit hutch, and the rabbit, when it finished its life as a pet for the children, was slung in the pot with some wine or vinegar – *alla cacciatora* – or cooked *in potacchio* or *in porchetta*. The latter is an odd recipe, so called because the rabbit is cooked in the same way as the *porchetta* or piglet. It is stuffed with wild fennel, garlic, rosemary and its liver and heart, then roasted in the oven, doused with white wine.

As for puddings, the Marchigiani hardly need them. They have the most splendid fresh fruits, with which they also make jams and preserves to cover their excellent *crostate* – tarts.

Salsiccia e Uova

Sausage and Eggs

In Le Marche there is a dish of *la cucina povera* called *coradella*, made with lamb offal and eggs. At La Torre, in Monteleone di Fermo, the chef serves *coradella* and also this dish, which is similar but made with sausage instead of lamb offal. He told me that it has as many variations as there are Marchigiane cooks: with a little tomato sauce, with garlic instead of onion, rosemary instead of thyme, and so on. This is the recipe for the dish I ate at La Torre.

SERVES 4

1 onion, chopped
extra virgin olive oil
6 pork sausages, removed from their
*   skins and crumbled*
75ml/3fl oz white wine

the zest of ½ unwaxed lemon
fresh thyme
6 eggs
salt and freshly ground black pepper

Heat some oil in a pan and gently cook the onion until very soft, then add the sausage meat and cook gently until browned. Pour over the wine, add the lemon zest and thyme and continue to cook, stirring occasionally for about 5 minutes until the sausagemeat is cooked.

Break the eggs into a bowl, add salt and pepper and stir lightly with a fork. Add the eggs to the pan and stir well. Turn off the heat and keep stirring until the eggs are scrambled.

Piccioni a Letto

Pigeons in Bed

A recipe from the Da Rolando Restaurant in San Costanzo, Pesaro Urbino.

SERVES 4

50g/2oz lard
1 small onion, chopped
1 carrot, chopped
1 celery stick, chopped
2 pigeons, plucked and gutted
1 glass of red wine

250g/9oz tomatoes, cut in chunks
1 teaspoon tomato purée
salt and freshly ground black pepper
500g/1lb 2oz maize flour
*a handful of grated **pecorino** cheese*

Melt the lard in a frying pan, add the onion, carrot and celery and fry gently until they start to brown. Add the pigeons to the pan and cook for a further 10 minutes, turning them until they are brown on all sides. Pour in the wine and leave to simmer for at least half an hour. Add the tomatoes and tomato purée, season with salt and pepper, cover the pan and leave to simmer over a low heat for 1 hour.

Meanwhile make a soft polenta with the maize flour (see page 81). As soon as the polenta is ready, transfer it to a serving dish. Carefully cut the pigeons into quarters and reassemble them into pigeon shapes. Place them in the polenta and cover them so that only their heads can be seen. Drizzle with the sauce and sprinkle with *pecorino*.

Coniglio in Potacchio

Rabbit with Tomato and Rosemary Sauce

Rabbit, chicken and fish are cooked in this sauce which has the trademark flavours of the region: lemon zest, rosemary, garlic and chilli. You can use a wild rabbit if you prefer, but remember that it takes longer to cook.

SERVES 4 TO 6

a domestic rabbit of about 1.5kg/3½lb
* cut into pieces*
½ lemon
2 tablespoons olive oil
60g/2oz unsalted butter
150ml/5fl oz dry white wine
1 onion, finely chopped
2 garlic cloves, finely chopped
salt and freshly ground black pepper

FOR THE POTACCHIO SAUCE
1 small onion
2 or 3 fresh rosemary sprigs, each
* 12cm/5in long*
the zest of 1 unwaxed lemon
1–2 dried chillies, according to strength
3 tablespoons extra virgin olive oil
400g/1lb canned chopped plum tomatoes,
* drained and coarsely chopped*
a dozen black olives, stoned

Wash and dry the rabbit pieces. Rub each piece with the half lemon. Heat the oil and the butter in a large sauté pan. When the butter foam begins to subside put in the rabbit pieces and fry on all sides until they are nicely browned. Add the wine, bring to the boil and boil for 1 minute. Turn the heat down and add the onion and the garlic. Season with salt and pepper, then cover the pan and cook for 20 minutes.

Meanwhile, prepare the sauce. Chop very finely together the onion, rosemary, the zest of the lemon and the chilli. Put the oil in a frying pan and when it is hot add the chopped ingredients. Sauté gently for 5 minutes or so and then add the tomatoes and a little salt. Cook over lively heat for about 15 minutes, stirring frequently.

Now that the potacchio is done, scoop it into the sauté pan with the rabbit and mix it with all the lovely cooking juices at the bottom of the pan. Let the whole thing cook together for another 20 minutes until done.

Test the rabbit for doneness by pricking the fattest part of the meat with the point of a small knife or a thin skewer. The juices that run out should be clear. Correct the seasoning before bringing the dish to the table.

I SALUMI MARCHIGIANI

THE PORK PRODUCTS OF LE MARCHE

Ciauscolo

This is a very soft *salame* made with 40 per cent fat pork meat and 60 per cent lean. *Ciauscolo* is flavoured with nutmeg, a little garlic and, sometimes, with orange and lemon zest. Finely minced, it is eaten fresh, about two months after it is made. *Ciauscolo* is the chacteristic *salame* of Le Marche, a type made only in this region.

Salame di Fabriano

This is a classic s*alame* of lean pork meat studded with fat the size of a grain of rice. Some *salame di Fabriano* also contains garlic. It is ready four months after it is made.

Lonzino

Lonzino is dry-cured loin of pork, often larded with lemon or orange rind. It is aged for six months. Lonzino is a very delicate product of pinky lean meat, surrounded by a thin strip of buttery fat.

Salsiccia di fegato

This is a soft sausage made with finely ground pig's liver and pork meat, flavoured with garlic, nutmeg and wine.

Prosciutto di Carpegna

After Parma and San Daniele, the *prosciutto di Carpegna* is reputedly the best. It has a stronger flavour than its two more famous cousins and a redder colour. The thigh of the pig is salted and then cured for a minimum of sixteen months, up to a maximum of twenty-four, in the area of Carpegna, between the cities of Pesaro and Urbino. *Prosciutto di Carpegna* is always sliced thicker than Parma and San Daniele.

IL BRODETTO AND OTHER FISH DISHES

Paolo Antinori is the head chef of an extraordinary hotel in Portonovo, just south of Ancona. The hotel consists of a converted Napoleonic fortress, built in 1810 straight on the sea to protect the nearby port of Ancona from any possible landings of British troops and make it impossible for British ships in the Adriatic to take provisions on board. The Fortino has been very cleverly and beautifully converted into a thirty-five-room luxury hotel. But the best thing about the hotel is its food. We spent four blissful days there in the summer of 2006. The weather was perfect, the sea like a millpond and the food excellent.

A few traditional Marchigiani dishes are cooked at the Fortino every day, plus local fish in the simple ways in which it should be cooked – grilled or fried – and a few dishes that are basically local but to which Paolo has added his own creative touch, with great success. Every day of the four days I ploughed conscientiously through the menu, and it was utter delight. I loved the *fritto di pesce*, a hillock of different fish crackling in its crusty light batter, topped with a julienne of courgette, carrot and onion, equally crackling. Even a grilled veal steak, not a food for which the region is particularly well known, was perfect, full of flavour and tender.

Paolo's two classic dishes of the region, stockfish and potatoes and *brodetto*, the fish soup of Le Marche, were both excellent. The stockfish, previously soaked for at least four days, is coated in a herb mixture, then cooked slowly on thin canes set on the bottom of a sauté pan so that the juices fall to the bottom. The potatoes, in small chunks, are added for the last forty-five minutes of cooking. The *brodetto* was excellent, thanks not only to the freshness and varieties of the fish but also to Paolo's particular touch.

Paolo came to our table with a bottle of red wine I was to drink with his *brodetto*. It was Lacrima di Morro d'Alba, which I had never come across before. I brought the glass to my nose and got a shock, a delicious shock but still a shock. The wine smelled of roses, the strong yet delicate smell of an old Bourbon rose. The smell was so incredibly pleasant that I didn't want to drink the wine. When I took a sip, I was amazed; the rose aroma had abated and the flavour of a fruity wine came to the fore. The extraordinary thing was that this wine was, as Paolo told me, the perfect complement to the *brodetto*. Roses and fish? I would never have guessed.

Brodetto all'Anconetana

Fish Soup Ancona Style

This recipe comes from Paolo Antinori.

SERVES 6

extra virgin olive oil
1 onion, chopped
1 carrot, chopped
1 celery stick, chopped
1.5 kg/3lb 4oz mixed fish and shellfish
(such as squid, dogfish, monkfish, sea
bream, skate, sole, plaice, John Dory,
red mullet, prawns, mussels and clams),
cleaned, heads and trimmings reserved

½ glass of white wine vinegar
a small bunch of fresh parsley, chopped
1 garlic clove, chopped
1 tablespoon flour
750g/1lb 10oz canned peeled tomatoes
a few slices of bread, toasted
salt and freshly ground black pepper

Heat a little oil in a large, deep frying pan and add the chopped onion, carrot and celery. Cook until the vegetables are soft. Add the squid, either cut in pieces or whole. Add the vinegar and cook for a few minutes. Add the fish heads and trimmings. Cover with water, add a pinch of salt and leave to simmer gently for 30 minutes. Remove the squid from the pan and reserve and pour the remaining stock through a sieve. Keep it warm.

Using the same frying pan, pour in a little oil and add most of the parsley and the garlic. Add the fish carefully, putting the firmer fish in the centre, then the pieces of squid, and arranging the rest of the fish with the prawns round the edge. Season with salt and pepper, sprinkle with a little flour, add the mussels and clams and sprinkle with more chopped parsley. Add the tomato sauce and the fish stock, cover the pan and leave to simmer over a low heat. Throw away any mussels and clams that don't open. Serve in soup plates, with slices of toasted bread.

OVERLEAF: *Fish for Brodetto all' Anconetana*

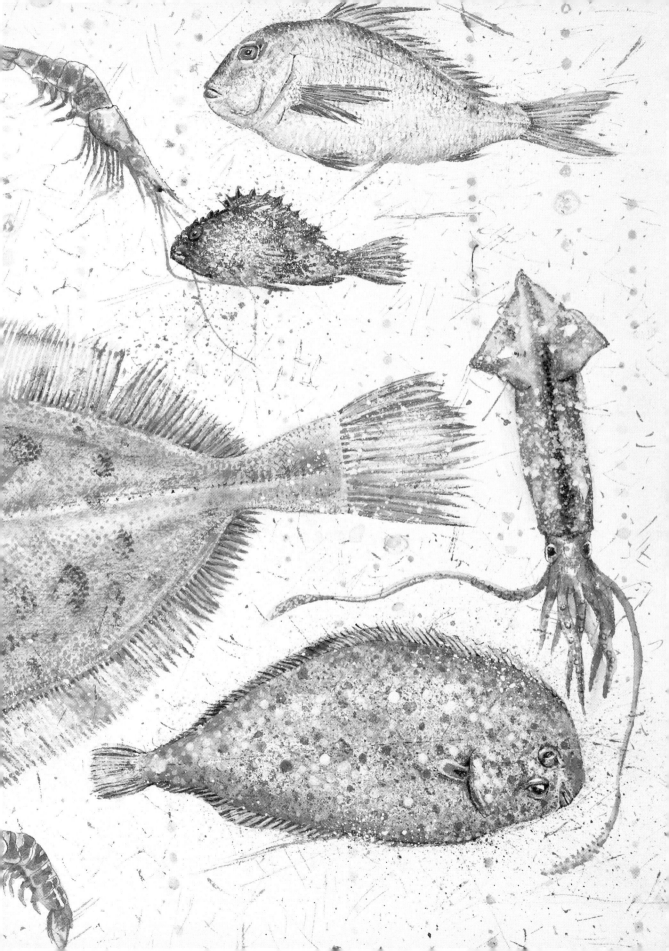

THE WILD MUSSELS OF PORTONOVO

And so it was that at half past eleven on an August morning in 2006 Val and I sat down at the Ristorante Emilia at Portonovo for mussels with bread and wine. It was wonderful, and we certainly did not miss the more normal *cappuccino* or *macchiato*. We were in Portonovo, south of Ancona, to talk to Franco Frezzotti, the man responsible for the Slow Food Presidium of wild mussels, which have almost disappeared everywhere else. Mussels now are usually farmed; in Italy 95 per cent of the mussels on the market are indeed farmed, at the expense of both flavour and nutritious value. The sea along the stretch of coast south of Portonovo is particularly free of contamination, and on the sea bed there is the ideal mix for a large biodiversity of fauna and flora.

While we were talking to Signor Frezzotti, the first of the five boats of the Slow Food Presidium came back with its cargo of mussels. This was the boat of the only fisherman who still catches his mussels by the old method of scraping the underwater rocks with a *rampone*, a long wooden pole with a net attached at the end. Carlo has caught mussels since he was fourteen, and by now, some fifty years later, he must have collected enough to supply every Italian restaurant. The other four fishermen, one on each boat, catch their mussels by diving with oxygen cylinders, a quicker job. It is, however, extremely hard work and no young men choose to do it. The youngest of the fishermen is forty-four.

It was a perfect day, sunny but not too hot, and I was enjoying this seaside resort that reminded me of those in my youth: rather old-fashioned, with the restaurants all in wooden huts lined up along the beach. We had a look at the trays of sole, small and slender, and of *cannocchie* – the French *cigales*. We went to watch the mussels being washed for the second time, the first washing being done straight away on the boat. And the most remarkable thing was that, in spite of the thirty-something degrees, there was no smell of fish, only the lovely smell of the sea.

'Shall we go and see the cook of the Ristorante Emilia?' Frezzotti suggested. So, some five minutes later (still not yet eleven o'clock) we were sitting round the table on the terrace overlooking the sea. We were with Marisa, the daughter of the Emilia of the restaurant's name and who is now in the kitchen, and Marisa's husband Franco, another fisherman, who looks like a sexy and lovable langoustine. In front of us were set three dishes of three differently prepared mussels: plain, with oil and parsley, and *arrosto* – covered with breadcrumbs and parsley and then roasted. There was also a bottle of Verdicchio di Jesi – the perfect match – and plain white country bread. It was the best elevenses of my life.

We talked food, of course, and I was hoping to wheedle a recipe out of Marisa when she said, 'Do you know that Prince Charles came here to eat spaghetti with mussels? I was so proud, and he had a second helping.' And she described the sauce. When I asked her with surprise about the lack of garlic in it, Marisa uttered this bold declaration: *'Nella mia cucina l'aglio non entra!'* 'No garlic enters my kitchen. I cook a lot of fish here and garlic would kill its delicate flavour.' Good for you, I thought, that you don't give in to fashion. Speaking about pepper, she also delivered a strong opinion. 'Never too much pepper; it is too strong. Better a touch, but just a touch, of chilli.'

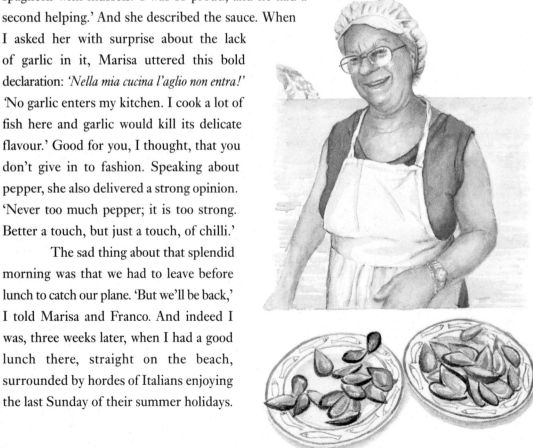

The sad thing about that splendid morning was that we had to leave before lunch to catch our plane. 'But we'll be back,' I told Marisa and Franco. And indeed I was, three weeks later, when I had a good lunch there, straight on the beach, surrounded by hordes of Italians enjoying the last Sunday of their summer holidays.

I started with Prince Charles's sauce, but I couldn't manage a second helping because I wanted to leave some room for the *fritto di mare*, which arrived as light as down feathers.

In the afternoon I went back to talk to Marisa and ask her for the recipe. Like most cooks I interviewed during my research, she uses canned peeled tomatoes for her tomato sauce because, they say, a good brand is more reliable than fresh tomatoes. Marisa was as generous with tips and information as she was with her spaghetti – a lovely woman and a very good cook.

La Salsa di Muscioli del Principe Carlo

Prince Charles's Mussel Sauce

This is the spaghetti sauce Marisa cooked for Prince Charles when he went to her restaurant some years ago.

MAKES ENOUGH SAUCE FOR 500G/1LB OF SPAGHETTI

2kg/4½ lb mussels
200ml/7fl oz white wine
2 glassfuls of extra virgin olive oil,
    preferably from Le Marche
½ onion, very finely chopped

a little chopped parsley
1kg/2lb 4oz canned San Marzano
    tomatoes
salt and freshly ground black pepper

Scrub the mussels and remove the beards. They should all be closed - throw away any that remain open when you tap them. Heat the wine in a large pan, add the mussels, then cover the pan and return to the boil. Reduce the heat and cook for 10 minutes until all the mussels have opened. Discard any that have not opened. When cool enough to handle, remove the mussels from the shells and chop them finely.

Heat half the oil in a large pan and cook the onion until very soft. Add the parsley and then the tomatoes. Cook for 10–15 minutes, stirring, until the sauce has amalgamated.

Meanwhile, put a large pan of water on to boil and cook your pasta for the time stated on the packet. Drain the pasta and add to the sauce. Stir in the mussels together with half a glassful of their juices and the remaining oil. Stir well to heat through, and serve.

THE SAGRA OF
THE MACCHERONCINI
OF CAMPOFILONE

Campofilone is a small town on a hilltop that rises close to the sea, dominating the fertile valleys of the rivers Aso and Menocchia and a long stretch of the coast. The panorama is vast and impressive. The town was rebuilt in the eleventh century over the site of a Roman villa with a fortified castle and walls.

A number of towns in Le Marche can boast similar architectural beauty and spectacular views. But only Campofilone can boast that it is the birthplace of *maccheroncini*. These are referred to in a correspondence of the fifteenth century by the Abbot of Campofilone as '*maccheroncini fini fini*' – very fine pasta that we would now call *capelli d'angelo* – angel's hair. It is also said that at that time the local women used to send *maccheroncini* every year to the pope in Rome. The recipe for this pasta is still the same, passed down from mother to daughter, a pasta dough made with the best durum wheat flour and eggs and stretched very thin before being cut very finely with a knife, not a machine, and dried on sheets of white paper.

In 1964 the people of Campofilone decided to dedicate a feast to their most famous product. So, during the first weekend in August, for four days, the town is decked out with flags and drapes and lights and candles, and in four strategic points of the town the four artisanal *maccheroncini* firms cook and serve tons of pasta to the hungry pilgrims. To be precise, 400 kilos of pasta and 300 of *ragù* are made every day, and 10 kilos of Parmigiano-Reggiano are used for the finishing touch. And litres of Rosso del Conero and Verdicchio, the two classic local wines, are consumed.

Val and I were greeted by the town's mayor and by Vincenzo Spinosi, whose father started producing *maccheroncini* in 1934. We religiously ploughed through dishes and dishes of *maccheroncini al ragù* made according to the traditional recipe, and came to the conclusion that we liked the Spinosi pasta best. This pasta is very good indeed, with a hard bite that defies its thinness. It is good with a meat sauce, as we had it, or

simply *al sugo* – with tomato sauce – but it is also excellent, as Spinosi suggests, with cuttlefish, whose ink turns the brilliantly yellow pasta into dark indigo strings. I very much like Spinosi's simple recipe below. With the *maccheroncini* we also had some *olive ascolane* (stuffed olives) and *crema fritta* (fried custard), both traditional Marchigiani dishes.

The Sagra dei Maccheroncini is totally secular – no saints or Madonnas or sacred relics or endless processions of black-clothed women muttering the rosary. A profane *sagra*, just to celebrate food and wine, much as the Romans used to do some 2,000 years ago.

Maccheroncini con Prosciutto e Limone

Spinosini with Prosciutto and Lemon

Sandro Spinosi, the maker of the best *maccherioncini di Campofilone*, has geven me this recipe, as easy as it is delicious.

SERVES 4

250g/8oz Spinosini pasta
75g/3oz/3 slices **prosciutto**
75ml/3fl oz extra virgin olive oil
45g/1½oz grated Parmesan cheese

15g/½oz parsley, finely chopped
5g/¼oz grated unwaxed lemon zest
1 ladle cooking water (approx
150ml/¼pint)

Cut the *prosciutto* into small strips and heat gently with the oil in a frying pan without browning. Cook the Spinosini in plenty of boiling salted water (approx 5 litres/8 pints) for 2 minutes. Drain and add to the frying pan with a handful of the cooking water. Cook for about 1 minute and remove from the heat before adding the lemon zest followed by the Parmesan cheese. Mix gently, adding the chopped parsley and, if necessary, more cooking water or a drop of oil. Serve immediately.

GIOACCHINO ROSSINI

Born in Pesaro in northern Marche in 1792, Rossini is widely acknowledged as the greatest composer among gourmets and the greatest gourmet among composers. Quite a few recipes bear his name, which generally means that they contain black truffles and *foie gras*. The most famous of his recipes is Tournedos Rossini, which he created with the chef of the Café Anglais in Paris.

Rossini died in Paris in 1868, and it was in Paris that he composed his *Otello*. He was taking so long to finish the opera that the impresario lost his patience and decided to lock him up without any macaroni until the opera was finished. *Otello* was finished in two months. Here are two other anecdotes about Rossini and his food. A lady went up to him once and said, 'Maestro, do you remember me? I was sitting next to you at that dinner where that splendid macaroni pie was served.' Rossini looked at her, thought for a long time and then said, '*Ah, si*, I remember the macaroni pie, but I'm afraid I don't remember you.' In the second anecdote he says to the soprano Adelina Patti, 'Madame, I have only cried twice in my life; once was when I dropped a wing of truffled chicken into Lake Como and once was the first time I heard you sing.'

Sale

PEPPA AND HER FREGNACCE IN BIANCO

Fregnacce are the cannelloni of Le Marche, and Peppa is the cook of the Pascucci Righi of Monteleone. She is ninety years old, still slim and attractive in her beautiful pink shirtwaisters, and she has worked for the family since she was twelve, first as a tweenie and then as a cook. Peppa is a talented cook in the traditional *marchigiana* mould. She cooked for us the most succulent rabbit *alla cacciatora*, a tender animal from the nearby farmer which she stewed in wine, flavoured with rosemary, garlic and grated lemon rind, the trademark trio of the local cuisine. With it we had beautifully roasted potatoes, crackling and soft at the same time, and stuffed, fried *olive ascolane*. The lunch finished with one of Peppa's *crostate* – tarts – made with a pastry that was halfway between cake and pastry and covered with her fig jam. In Le Marche they always add baking powder to their pastry, thus achieving a spongier result.

I went one day to help that delightful woman make *fregnacce* and she regaled me with lots of wise tips she had collected over seventy years in the kitchen. It was a treat and a joy to work with her. Her pasta was excellent, a little thicker than the classic Emiliana sort. With a slight apology she told me that now she makes her pasta with a machine. 'I am a bit old to make it by hand,' she added. But she still makes it once a week: lasagne, tagliatelle and *maccheroncini*, as the thinnest strands are called in Le Marche. She dries the strips of pasta over a thick cane, a sight that gives her pantry a festive look. Then she folds the strips up loosely and they are ready for the week.

For our *fregnacce* she got out thirty sheets of lasagne which she cooked, about ten at a time, in a large saucepan of salted water with two tablespoons of olive oil. We fished them out after about two to three minutes and immediately, still wet, we sprinkled on each sheet about two teaspoons of mature pecorino, two teaspoons of fresh pecorino and half a teaspoon of ground black pepper. We rolled each lasagna up and laid them, close to each other, in an oven dish, very generously buttered and sprinkled with cheese. We filled three dishes with the *fregnacce*, then poured over one or two tablespoons of the lasagne water. At the table we discussed whether a little melted butter would be a welcome addition. A little jug arrived at the table and a few drops were poured. Were the *fregnacce* any better? Maybe, but not so traditional any longer. And I felt that Peppa didn't totally approve of the suggestion by 'Il Signore' (Carlo Pascucci) about the added butter.

For four people you will need a pasta dough made with 200g/7oz of Italian '00' flour and 2 organic eggs, plus about 100g/3½oz each of fresh and mature pecorino and 50g/2oz of coarsely ground black pepper. *Fregnacce* can also be dressed with a plain tomato sauce, but these – *in bianco* – are the authentic dish, which predates the arrival in Italy of the tomato.

Peperoncino

IL LONZINO DI FICO

'Some people, having harvested the figs, remove the stalk and lay them in the sun. When they have dried a little, but before they become too dry, they put them in large earthenware or stone tanks. Then, having washed their feet, they tread them just as they do with grain and then they add roasted sesame seeds, anise seeds from Egypt, fennel seeds or cumin. Once properly mashed they form small, fat sausages with this fig mixture. They wrap them in fig leaves, they tie them with a reed or some herbs and they put them back on the wooden board to dry properly. When they are dried, they keep them in jars sealed with pitch' (Lucius Columella, *Res Rustica*, 165 AD).

And that is the way *lonzino* is still made now, in 2007 (apart from the treading with feet), as we were told by Gianfranco Mancini when we went to see him at his Cooperativa. Mancini is responsible for the Slow Food Presidium at Serra dei Conti, which also looks after the cultivation of the *cicerchia*, a very old pulse now being rediscovered by the cognoscenti of pulses, as well as chickpeas and other produce.

Lonzino is made with the white figs that are harvested in September just before the *vendemmia* – the grape harvest. The figs are finely chopped and mixed with chopped almonds and walnuts and the whole thing is flavoured with anise seeds, a flavouring much used also in ancient Greece and Rome. As Pliny wrote, 'Be it fresh or dried, anise is used for all conserves and flavourings.' Some *lonzini* are flavoured with *mistrà*, the local anise liqueur, and a few with chocolate, disapproved of by Mancini as a much later addition. He prefers to dip small lonzini in melted chocolate. But the best, he says, is certainly the original recipe as described by Columella.

The *lonzino*, wrapped in fig leaves and securely tied, keeps all through the winter and longer if preserved under vacuum. When cut it presents a lovely golden brown colour, speckled with the ivory of the nuts, and it exudes a pervading aroma of ripe fruit, enhanced by a touch of anise. It has a soft, pleasant texture emphasized by the nutty bits.

Lonzino is eaten as a dessert, just as it is, or dressed sparingly with a teaspoon or two of *saba*, another great product of the *'cucina contadina'* – peasant cooking – of Le Marche. *Saba*, or *sapa*, is the boiled-down must of white grapes, made also in Emilia-Romagna and in Puglia. It has a slight flavour of caramel, which is a perfect foil to the dried figs. Lonzino can also be served with cheeses, a semi-seasoned pecorino or a *caprino* – goat's cheese. Whatever you do with it, *lonzino* is a product worth being far better known, not only in Italy but also abroad. It keeps extremely well and it asks for nothing more than a sharp knife. The ideal pud for any host.

OLIVE ASCOLANE

If there is one kind of food that, in Italy nowadays, means 'Le Marche' it is the olives of Ascoli Piceno. They are large, of a straw-green colour, with an abundance of satisfying pulp to bite into and a sweet flavour, redolent of the Mediterranean countries. They grow in a small area – about 100 hectares (some 400 acres) – in the province of Ascoli Piceno, an area too small to satisfy the hungry demand of the market. Unknown outside the province up to about twenty years ago, the *oliva ascolana* has now conquered Italy as by far the best-tasting olive. And it is even more popular when stuffed and fried – a complicated but delicious method of preparing it.

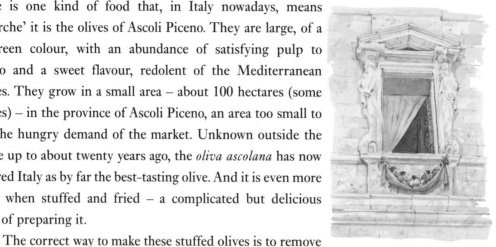

The correct way to make these stuffed olives is to remove the stone by cutting away the pulp in a spiral. This green spiral is wrapped around a walnut-sized amount of stuffing, and then the olives are lightly coated with flour, rolled quickly in beaten egg, dipped into fine dried breadcrumbs and finally thrown into boiling olive oil. They come out succulent and rich, with a fresh lively taste outside and a rich soft centre, the best preprandial snack to have with a glass of *prosecco* in the supremely beautiful square of Ascoli Piceno – or anywhere else, for that matter. The snag is that it is only in Ascoli Piceno or nearby that you can have the real McCoy, properly stoned and filled with the correct stuffing. The 'correct' stuffing varies according to each Ascolana family, but basically it must be a mixture of minced beef and pork, Parmigiano-Reggiano and grated nutmeg.

Val and I had these olives in quite a few different places, but on the whole those that Elena cooked for us at her *agriturismo*, the Villa Cicchi, were judged possibly the best, although those Signor Migliori prepared for us at his *gastronomia* in Piazza Arringo were also superb. At the Gastronomia Migliori we ate them with a bottle of excellent Pecorino, a white wine made with the grapes of the same name that grow around Ascoli Piceno. Pecorino, like the *oliva ascolana*, is a wine that has become better known only recently and it is certainly worth knowing.

At Villa Cicchi we had *olive ascolane* for lunch – and what a lunch! – as part of a stunning *fritto misto*. This is how *olive ascolane* used to be served in Le Marche before they became a preprandial snack. I asked Signor Migliori when and why the tender local olives had begun to be subjected to such a baroque treatment. He didn't know; apparently there are no references anywhere, but he thinks that it must have been in some wealthy family in the middle of the nineteenth century. But why? 'Just for one-upmanship, I presume.' And what upmanship it must have been to serve the traditional *fritto misto* garnished with these heavenly crispy balls.

Verdure Gratinate

Vegetable Gratin

A good and simple recipe given to me by Elena, the chef-patronne of the Villa Cicchi Agriturismo in Ascoli Piceno where excellent local dishes are served.

SERVES 4

2 purple aubergines

4 tomatoes

4 medium courgettes

2 red or yellow peppers

3 garlic cloves, finely chopped

a sprig of fresh rosemary, leaves picked

50g/2oz breadcrumbs

a bunch of fresh parsley, chopped

250ml/9fl oz extra virgin olive oil

coarse sea salt

Oil two roasting trays and a small baking dish. Cut the aubergines into 1.5cm/⅔ inch chunks and place them in a colander. Sprinkle them with salt and set aside for 30 minutes to drain. Halve the tomatoes and place them cut side down on a plate for the excess water to drain away. Cut the courgettes into 1cm/½ inch chunks. Cut each pepper in half lengthwise, remove the seeds and membrane, and cut each piece in half lengthwise again.

Preheat the oven to 190°C/375°F/Gas Mark 5. When the juices have drained from the aubergines, dry them on kitchen paper and spread them out on one of the roasting trays. Add the courgettes to the same tray and drizzle the aubergines and courgettes with oil. Salt the tomatoes well and place them in the small baking dish. Scatter with a third of the garlic and the rosemary leaves.

Mix the breadcrumbs with half the remaining garlic and most of the parsley. Add a pinch of salt and stir in the oil. Lightly salt and oil the peppers and fill with the bread mixture, then place in the second roasting tray.

Roast all the vegetables in the preheated oven for about 30 minutes, regularly checking their progress because they take different times to cook; the courgettes will be ready first, then the aubergines, the peppers and lastly the tomatoes, which should be well dried out. When everything is cooked, arrange the vegetables on a serving dish, sprinkle with the last of the finely chopped garlic and parsley, pour a drizzle of extra virgin olive oil over everything and serve.

THE HARVEST FESTIVAL OF CANDIA

By sheer luck, one day while I was having a blissful interlude at the hotel Fortino Napoleonico, south of Ancona, I heard of a festival taking place the following day in the nearby village of Candia. What intrigued me about this *festa* was that every year the villagers make a model of a church entirely out of sheaves of wheat, both *Triticum aestivum* (bread wheat) and *Triticum durum* (pasta wheat). I decided it was something I must see. Giacomo Mazzieri very kindly came to fetch me and off we went in his ancient rumbling car. Giacomo took me straight to see the straw models of churches, and there, in a large open hangar, stood slightly battered models of the Basilica di Pompei, the Duomo di Pisa, the Basilica di Sant'Antonio in Padua and, in the middle, in pristine condition, this year's masterpiece, the Basilica of Czestochowa in Poland.

Those churches, the painstaking work of the men and women of Candia, were there under just a roof, poorly protected from the weather and from the birds that love to eat a column today, a gable tomorrow. It takes a whole year to make just one church, which is then paraded through Candia during the last two weekends in August to celebrate the harvest festival. These churches are indeed works of art and amazingly are the exact copies of the actual buildings, made only with the stalks, ears and grains of the wheat. The Duomo di Pisa,

made in 2003, was looking rather tattered. But both the Basilica di Pompei and that of Sant'Antonio in Padua had not yet been so spoiled. I saw pictures of past works, like the Duomo of Milan with its hundreds of spires and the Cathedral of Ancona – just ten kilometres away – which all, alas, had succumbed to the ravages of the weather.

At six o'clock the Basilica of Czestochowa was drawn by a pre-war tractor up the hill to the parish church of Candia to be blessed, and then the feast began. And what a feast it was, with thousands of people gathering from all the villages around, ready for the Grande Bouffe and the dancing under the stars.

And the Grande Bouffe was grand indeed. Sandra Catena, one of the twenty cooks preparing the *pranzo sull'aia* – the feast on the threshing floor – described it to me. The first courses are the *boccolotti* (a sort of *maccheroni*), with a *ragù* of goose liver, heart, etc., and the rich *vincisgrassi* (lasagne). Then the roast goose appears – 400 geese each night! – served with potatoes roasted in the goose fat. There is also rabbit *in porchetta* (240 rabbits) and the great *fritto marchigiano*, plus four *porchette* – roasted piglets – just in case someone might still be hungry. The Bouffe closes with the *ciambellone del batte*, a simple sort of sweet bread covered with multicoloured sugar balls. I suppose the *ciambellone* is to mop up the wines, Rosso Conero and Verdicchio di Jesi.

We left at ten, far too early, I was told. Apart from the food, which was very good, what struck me was the kindness, generosity and warm hospitality of these people, a trait that I found all over Le Marche.

Frustingolo

Le Marche Christmas Cake

This is the Christmas cake of Le Marche, the recipe for which was given to me by one of my daughter's neighbours in the village of Monteleone di Fermo. When I made the cake in England I used *vin cotto* instead of the local *saba*.

500g/1lb dried figs
75g/3oz sultanas
75g/3oz walnut kernels, chopped
75g/3oz almonds, peeled and chopped
3 tablespoons vin cotto
100ml/3½fl oz clear honey
grated rind of 1 unwaxed orange

grated zest of 1 unwaxed lemon
100g/3½oz Italian '00' flour
50g/2oz dried breadcrumbs
a pinch of nutmeg
a pinch of cinnamon
120ml/4fl oz olive oil

Preheat the oven to 150°C/300°F/Gas Mark 2.

Soak the figs and sultanas in hot water for 30 minutes or so, then drain them. Chop the figs and put them into a bowl together with the sultanas, walnuts, almonds, and the *vin cotto*. Mix in the honey and the citrus fruit zest and add the flour, breadcrumbs and spices. Now pour in the oil and mix thoroughly.

Oil a 20cm/8 inch cake tin and line with parchment. Oil the parchment and spoon the mixture in. Cook in the preheated oven for about 1 hour (check after 50 minutes), until golden brown.

Crostata di Ricotta

Ricotta Tart

Another good recipe from Elena Cicchi of the Villa Cicchi Agriturismo in Ascoli Piceno.

FOR THE PASTRY
250g/9oz plain flour
10g/½oz baking powder
125g/4½oz unsalted butter
5 generous tablespoons sugar
1 whole egg and 1 yolk
grated zest of ½ unwaxed lemon

FOR THE FILLING
250g/9oz ricotta
110g/4oz plain chocolate, roughly chopped
110g/4oz shelled walnuts, chopped
1 small glass of white rum
3 tablespoons sugar
2 tablespoons dark cocoa (optional)

Preheat the oven to 160°C/300°F/Gas Mark 2. To make the filling, mash the ricotta with a fork and add the chocolate, walnuts, rum and ¾ of the sugar. Add the cocoa if you want the filling to be darker-looking, and put the mixture into the fridge.

To make the pastry, sift the flour with the baking powder and rub in the butter. Add the sugar, whole egg, egg yolk and grated lemon zest and combine well to form a dough.

Grease a 30cm/12 inch diameter round cake tin, flour it and tip off any excess flour. Roll out the pastry and line the tin, then fill it with the ricotta mixture and cover with a second round of pastry, closing the edges up well. Bake in the preheated oven for 30 minutes, then remove from the oven and allow to cool a little. Transfer to a plate and sprinkle with sugar just before serving.

Puglia

Frederick II of Swabia, a Holy Roman Emperor, King of Germany and King of Sicily, is said to have declared, 'It is quite clear that the God of the Jews did not know Puglia, or he would not have given his people Palestine as the promised land.'

Indeed Frederick chose to live a great part of his life in Puglia, the heel of the Italian boot. He had his dream castle, Castel del Monte, built there in the thirteenth century, a castle built in an octagonal shape, with eight octagonal towers. Whenever I visit Puglia, I see why this extraordinary man, who later earned the soubriquet of 'Stupor Mundi' – the Wonder of the World – preferred to live there rather than in Germany, the seat of his empire. Another of his soubriquets was 'Puer Apuliae'. The climate is kind, the countryside is beautiful, art is plentiful and the produce of the land is superb.

This large fertile region is best known for the huge number of olive trees that grow there. But almond trees also grow in profusion alongside the olive trees and that often brings about that perfect fusion of the two flavours in the oil. The two trees side by side create a beautiful contrast in the landscape, the feathery silver of the large olive tree so different from the strong green and sturdy round shape of the smaller almond. In the old days, when fields were small and all agricultural work was done by hand, the countryside of Puglia was dotted

with fields where not only olive and almond trees grew but also mulberries, fig trees, vines and persimmons, all sharing the same patch. You can still see some of these fields, often surrounding a *trullo*.

A word about these *trulli*, buildings that are unique to Puglia. They are small, round, cone-shaped buildings whose white stone walls come to a point at the roof. In times gone by the labourers shared the *trulli* with their animals. These strange buildings, which are a little like igloos, are mainly to be seen in the town of Alberobello and the surrounding countryside. Their ancient origins are not clear, but some historians say that they were built of unmortared stones so that they could be quickly demolished when the Spanish tax-collectors came round, and then quickly rebuilt. Some *trulli* are still used by farmers and a few are lived in by local people, but many have been transformed into holiday homes for rich Romans or Milanese or have even become smart restaurants and even smarter hotels.

Puglia has a very old history, and more than anywhere else in Italy, there is a palpable sense of antiquity. The people, the rhythm and traditions of their lives, and their delicious food, are today much as they were when Puglia was a Greek colony. The many and diverse foreign powers certainly left their mark, but never so deeply as to alter the intrinsic character of the place.

OVERLEAF: *Plumbago from Puglia*

The cooking, too, has been influenced by the various invaders. It has strong similarities throughout the region, in spite of its great size. That is because the same produce grows more or less everywhere, even if it appears on the table in many different guises. And this produce is always outstandingly good. Durum wheat for pasta and bread, wild chicory, rocket, onions, tomatoes, broad beans ... in fact, all the vegetables, pulses and fruits are first class, and the result is that the simplest dishes can so often taste the finest.

It is a cooking of the poor people, and fish also plays an important part in their diet. Still today the sea along the long Adriatic coast and the shorter coast of the Ionian sea is relatively clean. There are very few towns on the coast, not much industry and not too many tourists. All fish are found there, from the noble lobster and oysters to the plebeian sardines and mussels. With them the Pugliesi have created sumptuous dishes: *le tielle di pesce* – fish pies – a festive dish that is eaten hot, warm or cold. Meat makes a less frequent appearance on a Pugliese table, although I must add that the meat I had there was always top quality. It is usually lamb and kid, beef being less usual because of the lack of pastures. But who wants meat when you have all the best vegetables you can dream of?

And then there is the array of cheeses (see page 206), the multitude of cakes and biscuits and preserves and jams and all the other sweet things that were often made by nuns in the convents, as indeed they still are. The jams and almond cakes made by the nuns of the convent of San Giovanni Evangelista in Lecce are quite famous. You can still go there and buy them. Among other recipes in the convent registry there is a very interesting one for a *costrata*, a sort of pizza richly stuffed with caciocavallo, ricotta, eggs, spices and sugar, an ancient recipe where sweet ingredients are mixed with savoury ones.

The range of Pugliesi sweet things is extensive and they all show the Arab influence, just as the Sicilian sweets do. Of all these, the most complicated are the *cartellate*. At least that is how I found them when I tried to make them under the supervision of Paola Pettini, a marvellous cook who used to run a cookery school in Bari. The making of the hard wheat dough was already difficult enough. But then I had to stretch the dough very thin and cut it into 50cm long strips which I had to pinch every 3cm or so, fold over and roll round in a spiral, to make each *cartellata* look like a rose. These roses were fried in hot oil and then covered with hot honey or vin cotto to absorb the sweetness. As a final joke I was supposed to pile up all my messy oily things in a pyramid and sprinkle it with icing sugar. I didn't; I stopped and just admired Paola's beautiful sculpture, before destroying it by greedily eating it.

But the charm of this region is not limited to outstanding gastronomic experiences. There is plenty to see between one grande bouffe and the next. In the province of Bari the cathedrals of Bitonto, Barletta and Trani are impressively beautiful in their Apulian Romanesque style. A drive to the south brings you to Lecce, where a particular style of architecture – the Leccese style – flourished in the seventeenth century. It is similar to Spanish baroque, with extremely rich sculptural decorations. Taranto, a Greek city situated on its splendid gulf on the Ionian sea, has an archaeological museum that houses one of the greatest archaeological collections.

To all these attractions, you must add a very long coastline that varies from the rocky coves of the Gargano peninsula to the vast white beaches of the south. So my advice is 'Go now!' The Milanese have already discovered Puglia, and it will not be too long before the Nordic hordes descend on that blessed region.

THE TREASURES OF PUGLIA

Every time I go to Puglia I discover new treasures, be they artistic, gastronomic or natural, all great treasures. The first time, thirty years ago, it was Castel del Monte, the mysterious castle built by Frederick II of Swabia. On the same trip I was gastronomically bowled over by the taste of small octopus and sea urchins, eaten just like that, raw, with a squeeze of lemon juice, on Bari's quay. Then there was the spectacular mosaic of the Tree of Life on the floor of the Cathedral in Otranto, and the delight of popping a little burrata (see page 206) into my mouth. On the same trip I had my first 'ncapriata, the broad bean purée served with boiled chicory, and now every time I go there I must have it at least once. 'Ncapriata is for me the embodiment of the cooking of the region: clean and full of earthy flavours. This time I discovered the pork, beef and lamb of Puglia, which stand in comparison with the well-known beef of Piedmont and Tuscany, the lamb of Rome and the pork of the Cinta Senese breed in Tuscany.

We had the beef in Deliceto in the Lower Apennines of Puglia, close to Castel del Monte. We went there as guests of Vincenzo Mazzei, the local delegate for the Slow Food Presidium. The beef comes from the Vacca Podolica del Gargano breed, an ancient breed found only in southern Italy. The animals are raised outdoors and their meat is more fibrous, thus needing longer hanging, with a positive beefy flavour, ideal to be washed down by the wines of Puglia, full of body and strength. At the dinner given in our honour in Deliceto we enjoyed a carpaccio of this meat, and a *grigliata* – grilled steak, both excellent. I would have liked to eat more, but with eleven different antipasti, a splendid dish of pasta dressed with a *ragù antico di carne* – old-fashioned meat *ragù* – and then an impressive cheeseboard (*caciocavallo podolico*, goat cheese from Gargano aged in caves and served with chestnut honey, and others), it became an impossibility.

Among the antipasti dishes there was one in particular that caught my eye... and my palate. It consisted of two different kinds of salami – a chunkier dark one and a finer-grained second, and thin delicate slivers of the most buttery white *lardo* – salted semi-dried pig's back fat, just as good as, if not better than, the better known *lardo di Colonnata* of Tuscany. While I was enjoying these delicacies a vision of the lovely black pigs I had just seen up the hill flickered into my mind. I quickly dismissed it in the cowardly way we all do when we connect what we are so deeply enjoying with the sweet live animals in the fields, the suppliers of our pleasure.

They are indeed lovely, those black pigs. There was a young litter, nine black, one reddish blond and one spotted, all scampering around in their fields where they so much enjoy the acorns of the many oak trees. It is a very old local breed – Maiale Nero dei Monti Dauni – which was disappearing but is now being reared again in a few farms, of which the one we visited close to the majestic Convent of the Consolazione is the centre.

After the pigs, my meeting with the lambs was totally fortuitous. Val and I were admiring the façade of the Duomo in Altamura, which over the door has the most exquisite sculpture of the Last Supper. Christ is sitting on the left of the table, being kissed by a young Judas, who even in stone conveys the treachery he is committing. It was about lunchtime and to one side of the cathedral I spotted a sign saying 'Rosticceria'. I immediately dragged Val into it and there we saw an old couple, he a small and wiry man, flicking skewers under a red grill, skewers which his wife was threading with little bundles of meat lined up on trays. I immediately noticed that some of these bundles were tied with shiny 'string'. They were bundles made with lamb offal, and the string was the tiny intestines. I love *coratella* – lamb offal – but I could hardly put the bundles in a bag and go back to our smart hotel to eat them. 'Oh no,' said Cenzino, 'you go to the restaurant next door run by our son.'

And so, that night, there we were, enjoying the usual stunning array of antipasti, followed by bundles of different cuts and differently flavoured sausages. The meat was all from lambs of the Altamurana breed, locally reared lambs killed when still milk-fed. The remarkable thing is that the meat tastes of lamb, as indeed it should, in spite of the animals being so young. 'This is thanks to the pasture on which they roam,' explained Peppino Montemurno, who is the president of the Consortium of butchers of that area, a very knowledgeable, simpatico man who, with his wife, runs the restaurant. They prepare the antipasti, made mainly with vegetables, and then they serve the lamb bundles, sausages or grigliate – grilled chops – that the waiter (one of their offspring) goes and fetches from the grandparents. The family business is still thriving in Italy, thus keeping the family together, motivated by the pleasure of good food as well as the lure of good money.

Agnello con i Lampascioni

Lamb with Onions and Pecorino

This recipe is from the chef Raffaele Mazzarella, of the Ristorante Ballarò in Deliceto.

SERVES 8

*1.5kg/3lb 4oz shoulder of lamb or best end
neck of lamb, cut into chunks*
25g/1oz unsalted butter
50ml/2fl oz extra virgin olive oil
2 sprigs of fresh rosemary
150ml/5fl oz dry white wine

500m/17fl oz water or lamb stock
800g/1lb 12oz potatoes, cut into chunks
*500g/1lb 2oz lampascioni (see page 197)
onions, quartered*
6 tablespoons grated pecorino cheese
salt and freshly ground black pepper

Preheat the oven to 180°C/350°F/Gas Mark 4.

Put the butter and oil into a large frying pan over a high heat and add the meat and rosemary. Cook until the meat has browned, then pour over the wine and cook to let the alcohol evaporate, then add the water or stock.

Transfer the meat to a casserole, add the potatoes and the lampascioni, and cook in the preheated oven for 1½ hours, or until the meat comes away from the bone, checking the level of the liquid occasionally and adding a little hot water if necessary. Halfway through the cooking time, mix in the pecorino and add salt and pepper to taste.

When cooked, serve immediately.

OPPOSITE: *Red onions of Acquaviva*

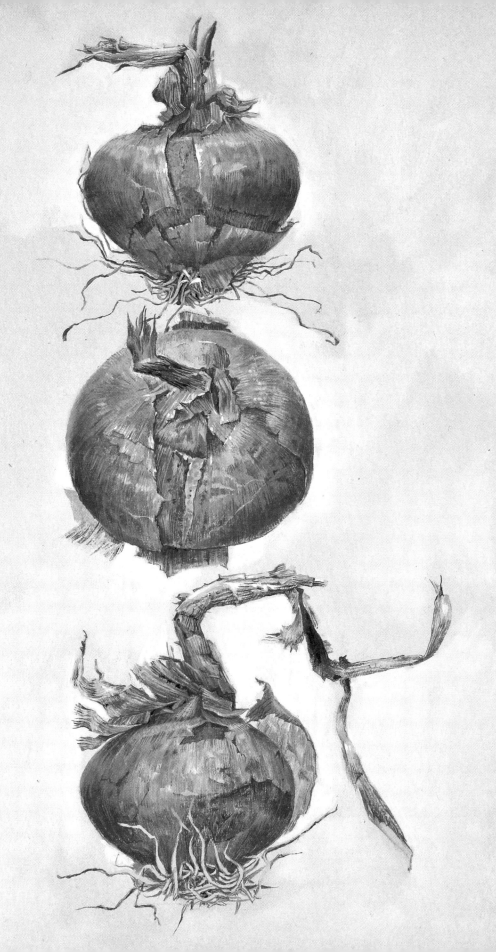

Involtini di Carne e Melanzane

Meat and Aubergine Roulade

A recipe from one of my favourite books on Pugliese cooking - *La Cucina Salentina* by Lazari Lucia.

SERVES 4–6

3 medium aubergines
1 garlic clove, cut in half
500g/1lb 2oz minced meat (half pork
* and half veal)*
110g/4oz breadcrumbs
110g/4oz grated cheese (half Parmesan
* and half pecorino)*

2 eggs
1 bunch of fresh flat-leaf parsley
extra virgin olive oil
salt and freshly ground black pepper

Slice the aubergines lengthwise into thin strips. Put them into a colander, sprinkle them with coarse salt and set aside for 2 hours.

Preheat the oven to 180°C/350°F/Gas Mark 4. Rub a mixing bowl with the cut side of the garlic and put in the minced meat, breadcrumbs, cheese, eggs, parsley, a pinch of salt and freshly ground black pepper. Stir well to combine all the ingredients.

Pat the aubergine slices dry with kitchen paper and lay them out a few at a time on a board. Make small balls of the meat mixture, place one in the centre of each aubergine slice and roll up. Lay the rolls in an oiled baking tray, drizzle with oil and bake in the preheated oven for 30 minutes, then serve.

Melanzane Ripiene

Aubergine Stuffed with Sausage, Pine Nuts and Currants

I was given this very good recipe from a local woman in the Gargano Peninsula. I like to add sun-dried tomatoes on the top of the aubergines as I think they go better than fresh tomatoes.

SERVES 4

2 aubergines, weighing about
*   450g/1lb each, washed and dryed*
salt and freshly ground black pepper
4 tablespoons extra virgin olive oil
1 large garlic clove, finely chopped
½ small onion or 1 shallot, very
*   finely chopped*
½ celery stick, very finely chopped
225g/½lb spicy **luganega** *or other spicy*
*   coarse-grained pure pork continental*
*   sausage, skinned and crumbled*

30g/1oz soft white breadcrumbs
3 tablespoons pine nuts
2 tablespoons capers, rinsed and drained
1 egg
1 tablespoon dried oregano
3 tablespoons freshly grated **pecorino**
*   cheese or Parmesan*
3 tablespoons dried currants
1 large ripe tomato

Cut the aubergines in half lengthways and scoop out all the flesh, leaving just enough pulp to cover the skin. Be careful not to pierce the skin. Chop the pulp of the aubergine coarsely and place in a colander. Sprinkle with salt and leave to drain for about 1 hour. Put 3 tablespoons of the oil, the garlic, onion and celery in a frying pan and sauté over a low heat until soft. Add the sausage and cook for 20 minutes, turning it frequently.

Meanwhile, squeeze the liquid from the aubergine pulp and dry with kitchen paper. Add the aubergine pulp to the pan and fry gently for a few minutes. Taste and adjust the seasoning.

Heat the oven to 190°C/375°F/Gas Mark 5. Add the breadcrumbs to the the frying pan. After 2-3 minutes, mix in the pine nuts. Cook for a further 30 seconds, then transfer to a bowl. Add the capers, egg, oregano, cheese, currants and pepper to taste to the mixture in the bowl and mix very thoroughly. Taste and add salt if necessary. Pat dry the inside of the aubergine shells. Oil a baking dish large enough to hold the aubergine shells in a single layer. Place the aubergine shells, one next to another, in the dish and fill them with the sausage mixture.

Cut the tomato into strips and place 2 or 3 on the top of each aubergine half. Drizzle with the rest of the oil. Add 12ml/4fl oz of water to the bottom of the dish. Cover the dish tightly with foil and bake for 20 minutes. Remove the foil and bake for a further 20 minutes.

This dish is best eaten warm, an hour or so after it comes out of the oven.

OSTRICHE, RICCI, POLPI AND ALL OTHER FISHY THINGS

The catching and cooking of fish in Puglia has a lot in common with that of the rest of the coast on the Adriatic or the Ionian sea, but there are some specialities and some aspects that are totally Pugliese. The *brodetti* and other fish soups are similar, although the fish soups of Gallipoli and Brindisi are richer and darker, thanks to the cuttlefish ink. In Taranto I have been served a fish soup that contained eel, good chunks of fat eel mixed in with the more usual rascasse, grouper, cuttlefish and langoustines. Pasta is often dressed with seafood sauces. '*Ma mai le orecchiette!*' I have been categorically told: 'Orecchiette are wrong with fish' – and that's that.

And then there is the usual grilled and fried and poached fish, plus the less common *pesce al cartoccio* – fish 'en papillote' – mostly made with the tasty rock red mullet. But there are two ways of eating fish that are uniquely Pugliese. The first of these is eating all crustaceans, molluscs, cephalopods and small blue fish raw, and the second is cooking the seafood and/or fish in elaborate pies called tielle.

I had my first experience of tasting raw octopus years ago on the quay in Bari, next to the fish market. I loved that morsel of chewy sea-scented fish with a squeeze of lemon juice. But I was entranced by the performance that preceded the eating. The polpetti – small octopus – are cleaned and put into a flat round basket, which the fishermen wave around in a special way to make the tentacles curl up. In the old days, I was told, this waving and curling dance was done by women, and it must have been a very attractive sight to see all those girls sort of belly-dancing along the quay. The bigger specimens are not curled up, just beaten to make them softer. Boiled in sea water, they make one of the most delicious antipasti ever.

Sea urchins are another heavenly morsel enjoyed there beside the sea. They are also used in spaghetti sauces. Anchovies, once the fish of the poor but now no longer so because of their scarcity, are also eaten raw, and most restaurants up and down the coast serve them. The smallest fish are either split open and spread out like a butterfly, cleaned, washed in sea water, then served sprinkled with olive oil and a little lemon juice, salt and pepper, or they are preserved in jars under olive oil and sent all over Italy and farther afield. All this raw fish is always accompanied by chunks of Pugliese bread, its assertive wheaty flavour counterbalancing the fishiness of the fish.

Sardines are popular too, cooked in many different ways. They are fried, but often with a stuffing of breadcrumbs, parsley, garlic and pecorino, accompanied or not by a plain tomato sauce. They are served in *tortiera* – baked in layers with similar ingredients to those in the stuffing – or layered with young sliced artichokes, all imaginative ways to prepare 'pesce povero'.

I must also mention fasolari, which are a raw favourite. They are a variety of cockle similar to Cardium edule but larger – about 5cm across. I am not keen on them, as I find them too chewy and rather tasteless. But I love the proper vongole – palourdes – and the mussels, which are both used for pasta sauces with or without tomatoes.

When we were in Monopoli, at its splendid fish market, Val spotted some red bivalve molluscs I had never seen before, which the stallholder called noci rosse. They were piled up next to some almost identical molluscs, but not red ones, simply called noci. I was told that they make a good pasta sauce with some tomatoes and chilli, just like vongole.

Last but not least there are the oysters. It is in Taranto that you can enjoy some of the best oysters of the Mediterranean. Taranto is a city on the Ionian sea founded by the Greeks. It soon became the most important city of Magna Grecia, renowned for its luxury in all fields of life, the table included of course. In Roman times, oysters were farmed in the gulf by starting the larvae on lentisk branches in the Mar Grande – large sea – and then bringing them in to the Mar Piccolo – small sea. Yes, Taranto has indeed two seas, or rather the large gulf and then an inlet. This inlet, the actual port, has less salty water, which makes the oysters more flavoursome; this is the opposite of most fish, which is better when caught in salty water. Today most Italian oysters still come from Taranto, but they are no longer as prized as they were in Roman times. This is because, for health reasons, they are kept for twenty-four hours in tanks of salty sea water, pumped from some 800 metres off the coast. But the best oysters and other molluscs now come from farms in Isidoro, a town between Taranto and Gallipoli. I have been told that the oysters are even exported to Holland and Belgium.

The *tielle* of Puglia are among the very best fish dishes. They are baked dishes of layered fish, rice and vegetables, among which onions and potatoes are always present. *Tiella* is actually the name of the large wide dish into which rice, soaked in water but not cooked, open mussels with one shell removed, tomatoes, onions, Parmesan and/or pecorino are placed in layers. It is topped with sliced partially cooked potatoes, the whole concoction being liberally doused with olive oil, of course.

The *tielle* show some of the origins of the food of the region. Rice was introduced to Puglia by the Arabs, and the way it is mixed with fish is reminiscent of the Spanish paella – which after all also has strong Arab origins. The Pugliesi have cleverly absorbed some of the food of their invaders. Mixing it with their own food and using their imagination they have created an outstanding cuisine of great originality and even greater honesty.

Tiella di Patate, Riso e Cozze

Potato, Rice and Mussel Casserole

The presence of rice marks this as a classic *tiella* from Bari. The recipe comes from cookery teacher Paola Pettini.

SERVES 6

150–175g/5–6oz long-grain rice
450g/1lb mussels
2–3fl oz extra virgin olive oil
1 medium onion, very thinly sliced
6 tablespoons minced flat-leaf parsley
225g/8oz ripe red tomatoes, diced, or
    ½ a 400g can of chopped tomatoes
900g/2lb waxy potatoes (4 medium
    potatoes), peeled and thinly sliced

450g/1lb courgettes, thinly sliced
75g/3oz freshly grated Parmesan or
    pecorino *cheese*
1 clove garlic, minced
225g/8oz ripe red tomatoes, thinly sliced
sea salt and freshly ground black pepper

Preheat the oven to 200°C/400°F/Gas Mark 6. Put the rice into a bowl and cover with water to a depth of 2.5cm/1 inch and set aside. Scrub the mussels thoroughly and debeard. If any mussels are open, shattered or have a cracked shell, discard them. Steam them in a lidded pan until they open. Discard any that do not open and strain, reserving the liquid.

Smear a tablespoon of oil over the bottom and sides of a 25cm/10 inch round oven-proof dish. Layer the onion slices over the bottom. Scatter over half the minced parsley and half the diced tomato. Layer half the potatoes and half the courgettes over this. Sprinkle the courgette layer with about half the grated cheese, along with salt and pepper to taste.

Place the mussels in their half shells on top, then drain the rice and distribute it in small handfuls over the mussels. Sprinkle with the rest of the cheese and the remaining tomato and parsley. Add more salt and pepper and the garlic and drizzle 2 tablespoons of oil over this.

Layer the remaining potatoes and courgettes on top of the rice. Sprinkle with the remaining cheese, adding salt and pepper. Use the sliced tomatoes to completely cover the top. Drizzle over the remaining oil, the reserved mussel liquid, and a little more salt.

Add boiling water to the tiella to come halfway up the sides. Place the dish, uncovered, in the preheated oven for 45–60 minutes, or until the potatoes are tender and the rice is thoroughly cooked. Serve immediately, or cool to slightly warmer than room temperature.

OVERLEAF: *Lampascioni: the bulbs of grape hyacinths*

ANTIPASTI

The two regions of Italy that offer the best antipasti are Piedmont and Puglia, two regions situated at opposite ends of the Italian peninsula. Of the two, I find the Pugliese antipasti lighter and hence more suitable in the summer, while the Piedmontese are the dream antipasti for an autumn day.

Any important lunch or dinner in Puglia starts with at least twelve antipasti. When faced with this spread, I often remember what Empedocles, the Greek philosopher and statesman of the fifth century BC, said when writing about Magna Grecia, of which Puglia was part: 'The western Greeks ate as though they would die the next day and built as though they would never die.'

The main emphasis of this glorious array is on vegetables, which are in fact the strongest feature of the local cuisine. Grilled sweet red onions from Acquaviva delle Fonti lie side by side with grilled red and yellow peppers, green and yellow courgettes, ivory and purple aubergines, all sprinkled with specks of garlic and tiny leaves of mint and glistening drops of olive oil. Aubergines and courgettes are very often stuffed with many different ingredients, as in the recipe on page 188, and most vegetables are also served deep-fried after being coated in flour, egg and breadcrumbs, a richer coating than the more common batter.

Bowls of cardoncelli fungi are placed next to bowls of lampascioni, a variety of wild muscary or wild hyacinth. The two are local specialities that can only be found in Puglia and of which the Pugliese are rightly proud. Cardoncelli have a very strong mushroomy flavour, similar to porcini, but they have a far firmer texture. They are often eaten raw (the Pugliese are lovers of raw food), following the example of the people who collect them in the dried, uncultivated terrain of the Murgia, where they are found. Often these people, usually women, eat them there and then for their *merenda* – snack – sitting among the stubble and the stones. Cardoncelli are sautéd in oil with garlic and parsley or, a better way, they are baked.

Emilia D'Urso, the producer of the best almonds I have ever tasted, took us round her wonderful estate, where the almond and the ancient olive trees grow among dry-stone walls, ancient ruins, fig trees, and huge agaves, and the undergrowth is covered with rocket, mint, fennel and other wild plants. All that land was once covered by forests, where red deer, stags, doe and wild boar roamed freely. Those were the ancient forests where Frederick II held his famous deer hunts with falcons. At the end of the nineteenth century, as soon as Puglia became part of the Kingdom of Italy, nearly all the forests were destroyed by order of the King because he wanted to eliminate the political supporters of the Bourbons who hid in the dense forests. And in the twentieth century what remained of the forests was ruthlessly cut down by local speculators to make room for industrial agriculture. On the D'Urso land, where industrialized agriculture does not exist, the feeling of an ancient land is overpowering.

Emilia told me that earlier in the year, at the weekends, they are invaded by people from the nearby town, who, forks in hand, come to dig out their beloved lampascioni and, while they are about it, collect rocket and fennel and all sorts of other wild herbs and greens. They wash the lampascioni, boil them, sometimes twice, to get rid of the bitterness, then finish them off in their favourite way. At other times they cook them on embers or they fry them, coated in egg and pecorino. They are also finished in a sweet-and-sour sauce with plenty of capers. In Locorotondo, a very attractive town in the province of Bari, I came across the most appealing way to serve them. The root was partly cut off, so that when the blanched and egg-coated lampascioni were deep fried in hot oil, each one opened up like a small rose.

A Pugliese antipasto will always contain a large platter of 'ncapriata – broad bean purée (see page 198) – surrounded by boiled chicory, dandelions, broccoli florets and all sorts of local seasonal greens. At the Masseria Panzo Piccolo in Acquaviva delle Fonti I once had peppers with this broad bean purée: they were long green peppers, known as sigarette, of which had been deep-fried. The 'ncapriata is one of the most ancient dishes known. Legend has it that Hercules ate a lot of it to find comfort after his labours. An enhancement of virility is also attributed to the purée.

As well as the vegetable antipasti there are the fish antipasti: raw fresh anchovies, filleted and dressed only with olive oil, lemon juice and salt, tasting of the sea from which they have just come, tiny octopus, raw again, their chewiness pleasantly contrasting with the softness of the anchovies, raw mussels with a squeeze of lemon juice or stuffed with the usual parsley, garlic and breadcrumbs plus a tangy handful of aged pecorino.

Large dishes of salami, prosciutto and whatever other local salumi there are stand side by side with dishes covered with various cheeses, among which burrata, caciocavallo, provola, mozzarella and goats' cheese are always present. Both are classic antipasto dishes of any Italian region.

And, after that, the proper meal begins!

Puré di Fave con Cicorie, Cipolle e Olive

Broad Bean Purée with Chicory, Onion and Olives

I had this 'Ncapriata (as this dish is called in Puglia) years ago at the Ristorante Gia' Sotto L'Arco and I still remember it as the best broad bean purée I have ever had. Here is the recipe.

SERVES 4

200g/7oz dried broad beans
200g/7oz potatoes
1 large red onion, finely sliced
1kg/2lb 4oz chicory
extra virgin olive oil

wine vinegar
50g/2oz large sweet green olives
2 bay leaves
salt and freshly ground black pepper

Soak the broad beans in cold water for 1 hour, then drain. Meanwhile peel the potatoes and cut them into chunks. Bring the potatoes and broad beans to the boil in a large pan of salted water, uncovered, over a medium heat. Reduce the heat to a minimum and leave to cook for 2 hours, shaking the pan from time to time.

After the beans have been cooking for 1 hour, put the onion slices into a bowl and cover with cold water. Clean and thoroughly wash the chicory. Bring a pan of salted water to the boil over a high heat. Cook the chicory until tender, crushing it with a fork while it's cooking. Drain and set aside to keep warm.

When the beans and potatoes are ready, drain and add 50ml/2fl oz olive oil, then transfer the beans and potatoes to a blender or food processor and make a smooth purée.

Drain the onion slices and dry on kitchen paper. Put them into a bowl and dress them with olive oil, vinegar, salt and pepper. Heat a little oil in a pan and gently fry the olives for 5 minutes with the bay leaves and a little salt. Serve the olives while they are still warm, alongside the onion slices and the broad bean purée, and accompany with the boiled chicory, dressed with extra virgin olive oil.

Cecamariti

I had this recipe from my friend the Baron Alessandro Bacile di Castiglione, who cooked it for us when we were his guests in one of his houses in Spongano, near Otranto. The odd name Cecamariti literally means 'blinds the husband', because, as Alessandro explained to me, the dish should be so hot that it can do that. He also told me that the traditional recipe contains fried croutons, which he has eliminated for calorific reasons.

SERVES 4–5

200g/7oz dried chickpeas
200g/7oz cannellini beans
110g/4oz frozen peas
50g/2oz green or brown lentils
120ml/4fl oz extra virgin olive oil

1 large onion, chopped
300g/11oz cherry tomatoes, chopped
2 teaspoons dried crushed chilli flakes
(or more to taste if required)
500g/1lb 2oz **cime di rapa** *turnip tops*
salt and freshly ground black pepper

Soak the chickpeas and the cannellini beans in cold water overnight. Next day, cook the chickpeas, beans, peas and lentils separately in fresh water until tender, and drain, reserving the liquid.

Put the oil into a large pan over a high heat and cook the onion, tomatoes and chilli flakes until the onion has softened. Add the drained pulses and peas and cook gently for about 30 minutes, stirring occasionally and adding some of the reserved cooking water if necessary.

Cook the *cime di rapa* in boiling salted water. Drain, then add to the pan with the pulses and mix well. Check the seasoning and cook for a further 5–10 minutes or so. Serve immediately.

THE FRUITS OF THE LAND

In the old days the best tomatoes came from Pachino in southern Sicily and from around Naples, the best red onions came from Tropea in Calabria, the best almonds came from Noto in Sicily, as did the best citrus fruits. But things have changed, thanks to the industrious and pugnacious Pugliesi, who decided they too could produce crops of the highest quality.

Some years ago we went to Vieste on the Gargano peninsula, a delightful fishermen's village, now of course no longer the same but instead yet another holiday resort. Never mind. You drive away from the coast and you are surrounded by unspoilt countryside and huge forests. I immediately noticed that on the more protected side of the mountains there were groves of citrus fruits, an extremely rare sight on the eastern side of the Apennines, which is at the mercy of the cold winds from eastern Europe. But there in the Gargano I saw orange and lemon groves, the trees in full flower or carrying fruits. These groves are called *giardini* – gardens – and they are indeed more like gardens than fruit groves, small and enclosed and sheltered by lines of ilexes and laurel. The two varieties of orange most grown here, called Duretta and Biondo, are both ancient cultivars whose cultivation has been promoted and helped by Slow Food in recent years.

The same can be said for the almonds that grow further south, in the province of Bari. We went to talk to the charming Emilia D'Urso, Coordinator of the Slow Food Presidium, at her beautiful masseria Pilapalucci, near Toritto, a town that could be called Almondville, as all the best almonds of Puglia come from there. The cultivation of the almond around Toritto is ancient, probably brought there by the Phoenicians. But, as the Count Domenico Viti, Emilia's husband, explained to me, the extensive cultivation started around 1870 with the unification of Italy. The forest, which covered a large part of that area, was cut down and the almond trees were planted. Almond trees are short-lived, about ninety years, so the trees we saw around the masseria were second-generation trees. The strongest cultivars are the oldest – the Filippo Cea and the Antonio Devito, which take their names from the late eighteenth-century agronomists who discovered them. These cultivars do not yield a lot of fruit, but what they yield is superb, with a subtle yet deep flavour that is far superior to the Californian almonds that have invaded not only Britain but, alas, even Italy.

I am an almond fiend, so I was delighted to sit there in the splendid vaulted living room of the masseria to have a comparative tasting and talk 'almonds'. Now Emilia D'Urso has also planted some modern cultivars. 'But I don't use those for my oil,' she said. 'For that I only use the Cea almonds. I use my oil for dressing the salad – only a little is needed – and for rubbing into my skin.' I looked at her lovely face and I thought the Cea almond oil does indeed do a good job. Emilia's oil, produced without any heating or solvents, is made only with selected organic almonds.

Almond trees are so much part of the Pugliese landscape, and in the spring they enrich it with their lightness and the romantic colour of their blossom. Almonds are used extensively in the making of cakes, biscuits and all other dolci. Another important use is caramelized in 'croccante' bars. If you go into a pasticceria and buy a small cake it probably contains almonds. Almonds are also stuck into dried figs, a gourmandise that claims its origins in Sybari, in nearby Calabria. Figs are eaten fresh, like all fruits in Italy, but because of their high sugar content they are also used in sweet-making. And, talking of fruit, I must not forget the grapes. Apart from the great quantity of wine made in the region, most table grapes come from Puglia.

The north of the region, the so-called Foggia plain, is also dedicated to the cultivation of the tomato, something that is relatively new. In the old days that part of Puglia was given over only to the raising of sheep. Some forty years ago vegetable growers started to irrigate the plain and to plant tomatoes. The tomatoes grew so well that they now compete with the famous ones of nearby Campania. During the summer the Bari to Naples motorway is chock-o-block with large lorries and smaller vans, all queuing to take their cargo of tomatoes to Naples. Most of the tomato industries have remained in Naples, while Puglia supplies most of the wherewithal.

But one industry is strong locally, that of dried tomatoes. It uses the same methods that are used in homes, the sun being the main drying agent. The same artisanal methods are also used to preserve vegetables under oil. These include mushrooms, olives and artichokes for making vegetable patés and sauces, as well as all fruit jams and preserves.

Another vegetable to be mentioned is the red onion of Acquaviva. This town in the province of Bari owes its lovely name – live water – to the fact that in the surrounding fields there are many sources of sweet water from a perennial subterranean vein. Also the soil is perfect for the cultivation of the onion, which was already very prized in the nineteenth century because of its sweetness. This red onion has a slightly squashed shape and a beautiful colour ranging from purplish carmine on the outside to pure white inside. Some of the onions are huge, even up to half a kilo. There is of course the usual snag, in that the yield is far inferior to that of any other variety of onion. But for me its taste is perfection in whatever way I eat it: cooked whole in the oven, sliced in fish *tielle*, roasted with lamb, or stuffed in a *calzone* – a folded-over pizza. There they mitigate the strong flavour of the other ingredient, ricotta forte – aged ricotta. They can be scattered on *focaccia* or, best of all, eaten just as they are, finely sliced with a dressing of olive oil and a blessing of that red ambrosia, the local Primitivo.

Also to be included among the fruits of this blessed land are the broad beans which traditionally have supplied the locals with all the necessary proteins. The broad bean is the most ancient pulse, mentioned in some manuscripts by Pythagoras, the first known vegetarian. Pythagoras's comments were, however, not favourable, as he, like all Greeks and Egyptians, associated broad beans with death, believing that the souls of the dead found their resting place in the beans. By Roman times broad beans were accepted and eaten happily.

The best broad beans I have ever tasted were those of Carpino in northern Puglia. The production is extremely small, as with all the best products, and the quality is superb. After being harvested they are dried in a particular way, on specially prepared soil, instead of being left to dry in the fields. The result is a broad bean with a very soft skin and a lovely buttery flavour, perfect to be eaten boiled and dressed with olive oil or puréed for the 'ncapriata (recipe on page 198), one of the culinary highlights of the local cuisine. In Puglia, oddly enough, broad beans are very rarely eaten raw, as they are in Tuscany when small and young.

As the Roman poet Martial wrote: If your pale broad bean is boiling/in your red copper pot/you can well do without/the rich men's dinners.

Rosata di Mandorle

Almond Cake

The best almonds I have ever tasted come from from the trees growing on the estate of Emilia D'Urso in Torrito. This is the recipe of one of the delicious cakes she makes with them.

6 eggs, separated
300g/10½oz caster sugar
300g/10½oz sweet almonds, finely chopped
a few bitter almonds, finely chopped

1 teaspoon of flour
a pinch of cinnamon
a few drops of vanilla extract
grated zest of 1 unwaxed lemon

Preheat the oven to 180°C/350°F/Gas Mark 4 and line a 25cm/10 inch loose-bottomed cake tin with baking parchment. Whisk the egg whites until stiff. Fold in the yolks and then the sugar. Once the mixture is thick, add the almonds, flour, cinnamon, vanilla extract and lemon zest. Spread the mixture out into the tin and bake in the preheated oven for 15 minutes. Once cooked, turn out on to a wire rack and cool before cutting.

OPPOSITE: *Almonds on the mosaic pavement in Otranto Duomo*

OLIVES AND OLIVE OIL

Every time I drive around Puglia I am reminded of Aldous Huxley's remark that if he were a painter and had enough time, for a few years he would only paint olive trees. The olive tree has indeed been portrayed in many paintings, mostly religious ones, sometimes as the symbol of peace, in others for pictorial reasons in order to contrast its feathery silver foliage against the backdrop of solid stone buildings.

The olive tree has also inspired many poets, from Dante to the twentieth-century poet Gabriele D'Annunzio. It also features in many popular poems, like this quatrain from Puglia:

> Della Puglia nativa
> l'olio d'oliva biondo
> che la salute attiva
> e insapora il mondo

Which roughly translates as:
> From the native Puglia
> the pale olive oil
> which promotes health
> and flavours the world.

Puglia is the quintessential motherland of the olive tree. An olive grove of old gnarled trees, as majestic as ancient oaks, is found next to one full of neat, silvery balloon-shaped trees, followed by another of dishevelled-looking olive bushes with contorted trunks, all intersected by white dry stone walls sneaking among them like large white serpents. Walk in those groves and you walk into the past, of which Puglia is more powerfully redolent than any other part of Italy.

In mythology the olive tree was the gift of the goddess Athena, who gave birth to it by striking her sword on the soil of Attica. From Greece the olive tree arrived in Sicily and Puglia around 1000 BC. The Romans developed its cultivation and began to classify the oil. The agriculturalist Columella (first century AD), who wrote that the olive tree is the most important tree, was the first to record the methods of cultivation of olive trees and of extracting the oil. These methods remained virtually unchanged until modern times, when motors replaced the water or the donkey that turned the stone wheels, and the pneumatic press made the wooden press obsolete. In Puglia, after the Barbaric invasions, it was the monks who replanted the olive trees and pioneered their cultivation. Soon merchants from all over Europe set up their warehouses in Puglia's ports, and olive oil from Puglia came to be appreciated everywhere, as indeed it still is today.

By the end of May the modest little flower of the olive tree becomes a tiny berry which by September has grown into a full-sized olive. Olives are picked at different times, from September to December. Some are harvested when still unripe and green, some fully ripe and purple and some a touch over-ripe and black. At this stage all olives are very bitter, yet with a pronounced basic flavour that is most appealing. The Pugliese quite rightly love their olives so much that they also eat them fresh, just like that, as soon as they are picked, in all their mouth-puckering but delicious bitterness.

I had them like that too for the first time as an antipasto at a dinner served on the jasmine-scented terrace of a masseria near Gioia del Colle. Our host had fried the olives in olive oil for a few minutes and then seasoned them with salt and pepper. In Monopoli the fresh olives I tasted were boiled and then again simply dressed, but the best fresh olives I ever had were at the hotel San Nicola in Altamura. Here the chef, Filippo Sardone, fried them in oil with chopped cherry tomatoes, a chopped fresh chilli, a chopped garlic clove and a generous handful of chopped parsley. We had them with plenty of that wonderful pane d'Altamura – but that is another story.

Olives, both green and purple, are preserved in brine, but most of the harvest is taken to the local frantoio. Here the oil is extracted from the olives as soon as they arrive, as it should be to make good olive oil. Puglia produces more olive oil than any other region in Italy and – as in all other regions – some is mediocre, some is good and some is excellent, with a slightly almondy flavour.

Olive oil is the fat that goes into all the cooking of Puglia and it is also used for dressing salad, boiled vegetables or grilled fish, or for making cakes and biscuits, butter traditionally never being used. More often than not, the Pugliesi add oil to the water in which the vegetables are boiled and then for good measure they add more oil at the table. On any Pugliese table there is always a bottle of olive oil, the best, of course, because to be added to any food at the end it must be the best. In many homes and restaurants this oil is 'olio santo' – holy oil. Why it is called holy I have never been able to find

out, since it simply consists of good extra virgin oil to which dried chillies have been added. But perhaps it merits the name because it gives the food on the table the final benediction. It does so, for instance, by livening up a dense broad bean purée, sweetening a bunch of boiled chicory, adding the flavour of the land to a grilled fish, enhancing a dish of spaghetti... in other words making any food more pleasurable.

To make olio santo some dried chillies are added to a bottle or jar of the best extra virgin olive oil. After a few days the oil has absorbed the piquancy of the chillies and it has become 'santo'. This olio santo is very popular in Salento, the part of Puglia that goes from south of Lecce to Santa Maria di Leuca, the most southerly point of the heel of the Italian boot. In Salento they say 'Il diavolicchio schiaccia la malinconia e mette in corpo dinamite ed allegria' – chilli crushes melancholy and brings dynamite and good cheer to the body.

THE CHEESES

No better lunch can be eaten in Puglia than bread and cheese. Simple everyday food, but what bread and what cheese! To sample some of those cheeses, Val and I went to visit the Caseificio Curci in Gioia del Colle. In the spotless room six men, all clad in immaculate white, were hard at work, mixing, lifting, folding, squeezing the pasta filata – plastic curd – to make mozzarella, burrata, provola and provolone, caciocavallo, caciotta and all the other Pugliesi cheeses. It is man's work, and strong men at that. In all my visits to caseifici up and down the peninsula I have never seen a woman working. 'They are not strong enough,' said Antonio Auricchio, maker of the eponymous provolone. 'Women just come in at the end, for cutting and packaging. They are far more precise and neat.'

The jewel in the crown of Pugliese cheeses is burrata, a soft pasta filata cheese, the production of which demands a great deal of expertise from the cheese-maker. He blows into the mozzarella paste to form a ball into which a mixture of shredded mozzarella and cream is poured. Quickly the neck of the ball is twisted and there is the lovely burrata, which can be small, like those Val and I popped into our mouths at the Caseificio Curci, or big, like the one I once enjoyed with a group of American journalists at Fasano al Mare. This cool white blob was so refreshing and cool against the sun-drenched background of a white beach lapped by an ultramarine strip of sea. Burrata must be eaten just like that, the connoisseurs say, maybe with only a sprinkle of salt and pepper if you insist, and if possible within forty-eight hours. The Shah of Persia is said to have had burrata flown to Tehran twice a week.

Caciocavallo is an ancient cheese made in countries all around the eastern Mediterranean, from southern Italy to Egypt. The long shaped cheeses are tied in pairs from the neck and hung for the ageing, which varies from three to ten months. They look like elongated flasks with tiny heads. Caciocavallo is mostly a table cheese, although the more aged cheese is also used for cooking. It is an excellent cheese, but the best I had was at the gargantuan feast organized in our honour in Deliceto, in Daunia in northern Puglia.

That caciocavallo was made from the milk of the Podoliche cows. This is a breed originally from the Ukraine, which was brought to Italy during the Barbaric invasions. It is now the breed of the Gargano peninsula, where they live on the hills in semi-wild areas. Unfortunately they yield very little milk and very few cheeses can be made, usually enjoyed in situ. Caciocavallo podolico is only a table cheese. After a few months of ageing it develops its special aroma of fresh herbs and bitter flowers scented with spices. It is indeed one of the most scented cheeses of Italy.

Teresa Curci was very proud of her mozzarella, the sort made with cow's milk, not buffalo's, which she said has its origins in Gioia del Colle. It is a good cheese that can compete with the more prestigious buffalo mozzarella. Caciotta pugliese is another great cheese, especially that produced in the province of Lecce, where it is made with a higher percentage of ewes' to cows' milk. It is a pasta filata hard cheese, with tiny eyes and a pale buff yellow colour. It is aged for about twenty days and it is then at its best, with its intense yet delicate flavour.

Another important cheese of Puglia is provolone, a semi-fat cows' milk cheese of the same pasta filata as caciocavallo. Its many shapes vary a lot, from small provoline of about 0.5kg in the shape of a pear, or a drop, to cheeses of about 5kg shaped like a rounded cone or a flask, to the very big shapes of more than 10kg looking like a huge salame. In the province of Foggia they also make little provoline in the shape of horses, called cavallucci.

And then of course there is the humble ricotta, which to be correct is not a cheese, but a by-product of cheese-making. It is in fact made from the whey of the cheese. The best ricotta are those made with ewe's milk. But any ricotta, fresh and still lukewarm, just out of its basket, is a treat even for the most demanding gourmet.

PANE E PASTA

These two keystones of Italian cooking, bread and pasta, find their apogee in Puglia. This is partly due to the fact that the best durum wheat grows in the Pugliese plateau called il Tavoliere and partly because of the strong local tradition of good-quality food. When I was a child, every time my mother, a very good cook and an even more discerning eater, ate a new kind of bread she would say, 'Good, but not as good as il pane di Altamura.' I found it a boring refrain. But later in life, when I too became a discerning eater, I saw what she meant. The bread of Altamura is the quintessential bread, with its chewy crumbs tasting of wheat and its thick crusty crust.

In the ancient past the Greek bakers were famous. Their tradition of bread-making was passed on in the most Greek of all Italian regions and it still exists there some two and a half millennia later. Altamura is the centre of bread-making and its bread has now been granted the much sought-after DOP status. It is made from durum wheat, very finely ground, with a high proportion of water to flour. It is leavened with sour dough which has been passed down through the generations.

In Altamura Val and I went to see Carlo and Grazia Picerno at their bakery, La Panetta. Carlo had been hard at work since four o'clock, though actually I should say since the previous Sunday. He only goes home on Saturday afternoons. He sleeps in the bakery, kept warm by his large stone oven, so that he can look after his oven and the bread, of which he is so rightly proud. The flour Carlo uses is finely ground durum wheat. The round shapes are large, ranging from 1kg even up to 10kg, following the local tradition. The dough is given three risings and then baked in the large stone oven heated by oak, which, being hard, allows the water to evaporate slowly and the bread to cook properly without burning the crust.

Grazia cut a loaf and gave us a piece and its taste filled me with delight, perhaps even more so than later when I tasted the milk biscuits she produced for us (see page 211) . Carlo also makes savoury bread and pizza, although I could see that his heart is in the traditional Pugliese loaf.

We left the shop with a bag of *biscotti al latte* and a bag of *taralli*, my favourite preprandial snacks. *Taralli* are savoury biscuits shaped rather like a knot and are flavoured with fennel seeds or chilli. The secret of the best taralli is that they are first blanched and then baked. They are now one of the most popular snacks in Italy, made industrially everywhere, but the artisanal *taralli* you eat in Puglia, made according to the ancient golden rules, are unforgettable.

The next day, after the pane, we went to see pasta being made. Our demonstrator was a lovely local lady, Cecilia Sardone, who lives about ten minutes from the hotel, which gave us the opportunity to walk around another part of the extremely beautiful town of Altamura. Cecilia welcomed us with the usual warmth of the southerners and led us into her spotlessly clean kitchen, which on that day of late October was full of the most radiant warm sunshine. She had a bag of flour on the table and a jug of hot water and off she went, mixing and kneading and rolling and shaping the dough. Val and I had come to learn how to do it.

I know perfectly well that I cannot make orecchiette, however many times I try. I tried again with Cecilia and – quite rightly – she declared, '*Ma che schifezza*!' But, what a mess! Orecchiette or, for that matter, all other Pugliese pasta, is made with durum wheat semolina and water, rather than soft wheat flour and eggs like the dough from the north that I'm used to making. The durum wheat dough is extremely difficult to make and shape, at least for me. Watching Cecilia at work, you'd think it was child's play. That day she made orecchiette, shaping the knob of dough with her thumb, capunti, shaping them with two fingers, and capuntini, the smaller edition. Not only were the little shapes perfect but her speed was phenomenal. Then she took us down the road, *a bracetto* – arm in arm – proud to be the teacher of these two exotic ladies, to her greengrocer to buy the turnip tops for the orecchiette. My regret was that we never ate those orecchiette. I'm sure Cecilia would have produced a lovely dish, but we had to move on to our next port of call.

There are many other pasta shapes that Cecilia didn't have time to show us, like *ferricelli*, made with knitting needles, or *sagne cannullate*, long spirals made with wooden sticks. All these shapes are matched with the right sauces. Broccoli and cauliflower with this shape, lamb *ragù* with that, cardoncelli mushrooms with the other, vongole and sea urchins with yet another – but *never* with orecchiette, I was strongly warned.

Orecchiette alle Cime di Rapa e Peperoncino

Orecchiette with Turnip Tops and Chilli

Cime di rapa or turnip tops are in season from around September to January; if you can't find turnip tops, use broccoli instead. This recipe is by Giorgio Locatelli from his book *Made in Italy*.

SERVES 4

3 small bunches of **cime di rapa**
  (turnip tops)
5 tablespoons extra virgin olive oil
2 garlic cloves, thinly sliced
2 medium long red chillies, deseeded (leave the
  seeds in if you want more heat) and thinly sliced

400g/13oz dried orecchiette
2 anchovy fillets
salt and freshly ground
  black pepper

Take the leaves and florets of the cime di rapa from their stalks and blanch them in boiling salted water for about a minute, just to take away some of their bitterness. Drain and squeeze to remove the excess water. Chop very finely.

Warm half the olive oil in a large sauté pan, add the garlic and chilli and gently cook them without allowing them to colour (don't let the garlic burn or it will taste bitter). Then add the cime di rapa and toss around. Add another tablespoon of olive oil.

Meanwhile, bring a large pan of salted water to the boil, add the orecchiette and cook for a minute less than the time given on the packet until al dente.

While the pasta is cooking, ladle out a little of the cooking water and add to the pan containing the cime di rapa. Then turn down the heat and add the anchovies as well. Let them dissolve, without frying them, stirring them all the time. Taste and season of necessary – remember that the anchovies will add their own saltiness.

When the pasta is cooked, drain, reserving the cooking water, and add the pasta to the pan containing the sauce. Toss around for 2–3 minutes so that the cime di rapa cook a little more and begin to cling to the pasta. Add the rest of the olive oil, toss well to coat and serve.

OVERLEAF: *Pane di Altamura and the Last Supper from the Duomo, Altamura*

Tria e Cicieri

Tagliatelle Soup with Chickpeas

SERVES 4–6

300g/11oz chickpeas
a pinch of bicarbonate of soda
a few bay leaves
1 garlic clove, chopped
1 onion, chopped
1 celery stick, chopped

1 carrot, chopped
3 ripened tomatoes, chopped
extra virgin olive oil
400g/14oz fresh tagliatelle
salt and freshly ground black pepper

Soak the chickpeas overnight in water with a pinch of bicarbonate of soda and a handful of coarse salt. Rinse them thoroughly and put into a pan with plenty of salted water and a bay leaf. Bring to the boil, then reduce the heat and simmer for 15 minutes. Add the garlic, onion, celery, carrot and tomatoes and leave to simmer gently for about 1 hour.

Heat some oil in a frying pan and fry half the tagliatelle. Cook the other half in boiling salted water. Heat a second frying pan or large saucepan over a medium heat. When the chickpeas and vegetables are tender, put them into in the frying pan and stir in the fried and boiled tagliatelle and a little olive oil. Sprinkle with black pepper and serve.

Grazia's Milk Biscuits

MAKES APPROX 50

250g/9oz Italian '00' flour
1 level teaspoon baking powder
1 large egg, beaten

90g/3oz sugar
4 tablespoons light olive oil
about 2 tablespoons milk

Preheat the oven to 180°C/350°F/Gas Mark4. Put all the ingredients into a bowl and mix together until a soft dough is formed. Roll out on a lightly floured board and cut out the biscuits using a 5cm/2 inch round cutter. Place on a non-stick baking sheet and bake in the oven for 10–15 minutes until golden brown. Cool on a wire rack.

Sardinia

'Lost between Europe and Africa
and belonging to nowhere.'
So wrote D. H. Lawrence in his
book *Sea and Sardinia*, and so
it seems to me even now, almost
ninety years later.

You arrive on the island, and as soon as you begin to look around, to talk to the locals and to move from place to place, you realize you are not really in Italy, nor in Africa, nor in any other familiar place. Sardinia is a fascinating world of its own, full of mystery. Invaded by hordes of foreigners, from the Phoenicians and the Romans to the Spanish and the Piedmontese, it has always kept its strong identity and remained untouched by the habits and customs of the invaders. In fact these foreign invaders never managed to conquer the whole island. Even the Romans, who settled mainly in the south, and were there for over four centuries, never conquered the Barbagia, the wildest and highest part of Sardinia.

Even Sardinia's most important ruins, the *nuraghi*, are a mystery. They are the remains of conical buildings made of huge stones, sometimes standing alone in the middle of ancient olive groves, sometimes in pairs, sometimes in groups. They date from around 1500 BC, the time of the Egyptian civilization, but unlike in Egypt, nothing written has ever been found to throw light on the mystery. Nowadays the archaeologists think the *nuraghi* were the homes of the tribal chiefs, built to defend the tribe and shelter it in case of attack.

Something that links these prehistoric ruins with the present is the large ovens that can be seen in some *nuraghi*. Those ancient tribes must have baked the same bread that their successors bake today, bread that is the most symbolic food of the island (see page 238). The cooking of this rugged island still maintains an archaic character, due mainly to the strong

attachment of its inhabitants to the traditions of their
elders, and to their relative poverty. They still have an
economy based mostly on agriculture and sheep-breeding. The
invaders – the Genoese, the Spanish and, in the north, the Piedmontese – only influenced the
cooking around the coasts. Inland, the cooking is still the cooking of the shepherds: a lot of
bread and cheese and pasta, some lamb and kid and rabbit, plus wild plants and herbs for
vegetables and flavourings. These herbs are the ideal fodder for the 3,500,000 sheep that roam
around the island (two and a half sheep for each Sardinian!), and they impart to the local
pecorini that intense herby flavour that makes these Sardinian cheeses
especially delicious. All meat is roasted on the spit. The
animal is cooked whole over a fire of aromatic
woods, among which myrtle is essential.

In the depths of the Barbagia you
might still come across an antique method of
cooking a lamb, kid, piglet or rabbit. Alas,
I never met it during my several visits to the
island, but I hope it hasn't totally died out.
Apparently it was started by bandits up in

the mountains, who had to eat what they could steal without their presence being given away by plumes of smoke billowing up into the sky. A hole is dug and lined with stones which are heated until they are red hot. The animal, salted and flavoured with wild herbs, is pushed into the hole, which is covered with hot stones. Nowadays, to speed up the cooking, wood is placed over the top and set on fire. The expert shepherd knows when the animal is ready to be taken out. This cooking is called *a carraxiu*, meaning 'buried' in Sardinian dialect.

The writer Charles Edwards was lucky enough to eat a boar cooked *a carraxiu*. In his book *Sardinia and the Sards*, published in 1889, he wrote, 'Here then, we ate a wild boar, shot in the precincts of the mine that very morning and baked in a ground oven by a Sard cook. With lettuces, bread, cheese, olives, oranges, wine of Tortoli, and the mountain air, it was a feast for an alderman.' A festive *carraxiu* might consist of an animal containing another, which contains another, which contains another, and so on. I have been told it is still done – from a bullock to a thrush – in the province of Nuoro, where a cobbler is called in to do the sewing up. So the fashionable modern way of stuffing a turkey with a smaller bird and then one smaller still is nothing but an archaic method of cooking that has existed on this island since time immemorial.

Oddly enough for an island with over 1,300 kilometres of coastline, Sardinia is not a land of fishermen. Of course, fish is now the restaurant food par excellence all around the island, but traditionally it is only in Alghero and around the north coast, and in and around Cagliari, the capital, in the south, that fish is a traditional dish. Alghero, a beautiful town of Catalan origin on the north-west coast, boasts the best crustaceans and cephalopods, and dishes such as *cassola*, a rich fish stew, and *pesce in scabeche*, fried grey mullet in a vinegary tomato sauce. Down in the south I have seen and eaten huge *grigliate di pesce* – grilled fish, containing a selection of fish I have not seen anywhere else. There they also grill long slender eels, which they spike in a serpentine fashion on skewers, forming a beautiful shiny blue pattern.

But the best place for fish is the island of San Pietro, off the western coast of Sardinia. This island has an odd history. In the eighteenth century it was given by the Savoys to the descendants of Genoese families who were evicted from Tunisia, where they had been forced to settle in the sixteenth century. So in San Pietro the dialect is Genoese, not

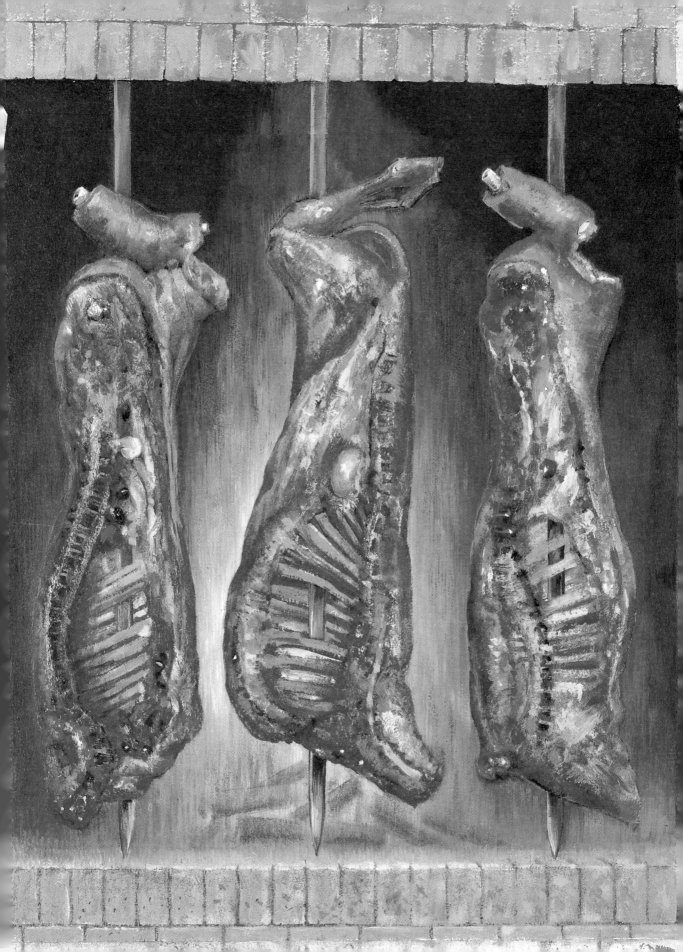

Sardinian, the houses of Carloforte, the capital, are similar to those of Camogli in Liguria, and the food shows its original provenance, often with a touch of Arab influence. The *cascà* is similar to couscous, and the *farinate* and *panisse* – chickpea dishes – are as in Liguria. I had a *cappon magro* there that was the exact replica of the authentic Genoese one. On the island of San Pietro there are *tonnare*, where tuna fish is caught, much of which is exported to Japan. It is also preserved on the spot and, if you tasted that, you would know what good preserved tuna is really like and what a lot of rubbishy tinned stuff there is on the market. But of all fishy things, the great Sardinian product is *bottarga*, which is certainly worth a special tribute (see page 226).

The savage beauty of the island of Sardinia is exemplified by the huge masses of jade green prickly pears that dominate the countryside, so striking, untamed and untamable.

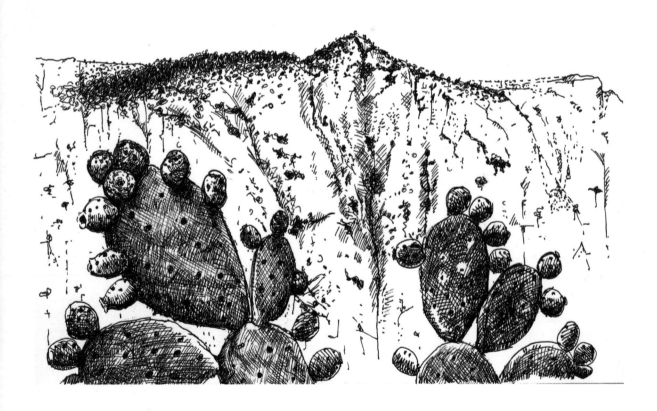

Agnello alla Sarda

Sardinian Lamb

I have a friend in Sardinia, Maria Clara de'Montis, who is one of the best cooks I know. Maria Clara is also extremely knowledgeable about the cooking of her beloved island. This recipe for lamb is a perfect one-pot dish.

SERVES 4

2 large potatoes
1.2 kg/2lb 12oz lamb shoulder, cut into
   8 pieces
4 large spring onions
4 garlic cloves
2 stock cubes

1 glass of red wine
1 glass of water
1 ladle of oil
a small bunch of fresh parsley
freshly ground black pepper

Preheat the oven to 150°C/300°F/Gas Mark 2.

    Halve the potatoes, cook them in boiling salted water for 5 minutes, and drain. Put them into a large baking tray or ovenproof dish with all the other ingredients. Cover with kitchen foil, cook in the preheated oven for 1 hour, then remove from the oven and serve.

OPPOSITE: *Prickly pears at Su Gologogne*

Tagliata di Dentice

Baked Dentex Fillets with Parsley Sauce

SERVES 4

The dressing for this recipe is a favourite of Giuseppe Ercole, the grandson of the founder of Sacla', and he prepares it to serve with his catch of the day. Its fresh flavour perfectly complements the delicate flavour of the fish.

4 dentex fillets, about 2kg/4lb (total weight)
extra virgin olive oil
2 teaspoons green or pink peppercorns, coarsely crushed

FOR THE PARSLEY SAUCE
75ml/3fl oz extra virgin oil
25g/1oz chopped fresh parsley
1 garlic clove
1 hard-boiled egg, finely chopped
2–3 teaspoons lemon juice
salt and freshly ground black pepper

TO SERVE
watercress
vinaigrette dressing

Put the fish fillets into a dish and rub them all over with olive oil and crushed peppercorns. Set the fish aside for 3–4 hours.

Meanwhile make the parsley sauce. Mix all the ingredients together and season to taste, adding more lemon juice if necessary. Set aside.

Preheat the oven to 180°C/350°F/Gas Mark 4. Heat 1 tablespoon of olive oil in a large non-stick frying pan and fry the fillets skin side down over a high heat for 2 minutes until the skin is crispy, then turn over and cook for another 1–2 minutes. Transfer them to an ovenproof dish or a baking tin and cook in the oven for 15 minutes. The fish will be golden on the outside and lightly pink inside – the flesh should still be moist.

Slice the fillets and serve with the parsley sauce and a bowl of watercress, lightly dressed with a vinaigrette.

Cernia in Salsa

Grouper with Tomato Sauce

We had this grouper in the Osteria Graf in Oristano. It was a delicious meal which started with Bottarga and finished with my favourite Sardinian *dolce* Sebadas (see page 243). Instead of the grouper you can use a large grey mullet as an alternative.

SERVES 4

olive oil
4 x 200g/7oz fillets of grouper
1 fresh red chilli, finely chopped
1 glass of **vernaccia** wine

salt and freshly ground black pepper
500g/1lb 2oz ripe tomatoes, peeled and
  chopped
a handful of fresh parsley, chopped

Heat a drizzle of olive oil in a frying pan and add the fish and the chilli. Cook for 2–3 minutes, until the fish has a rich golden colour. Pour in the wine and season with salt and pepper, then add the tomatoes to the pan and cook for 20 minutes. Serve sprinkled with fresh chopped parsley.

PORCEDDU

The crown jewel of Sardinian cooking, *porceddu,* is a piglet of Sardinian breed, still milk-fed. The ideal weight is 7 to 8kg, and it should certainly be no heavier than 15kg. It can be cooked on the spit, *a carraxiu* (in the ground) or on a barbecue. I have eaten *porceddu* several times in Sardinia, but the ones I had at a party near Monastir, north of Cagliari, and at the Su Gologone hotel were the best. Both were cooked on the spit, which connoisseurs say is the best way.

The *porceddu* of Monastir had been cooked by the butcher in Pula, in southern Sardinia, and the day after the party I went to see him. His shop was full of women, buying 200g of this, 100g of that, everything to be sliced, minced, beaten, or cut this way or that way, all under the hawk-eyed supervision of the customer. When it was my turn I introduced myself as '*una giornalista inglese*' and everybody stood silent and stared at me, surprised that I was able to speak a word of Italian at all, let alone perfectly. I asked the butcher how he made the delicious *porceddu* I had had the night before, and he said, 'First you must buy a piglet of the Sardinian breed no heavier than ten kilograms. Then you must salt it with Sardinian salt.' I intervened and said, 'What about Sicilian salt, which is easier to find?' 'Ah no, Signora. Sicilian salt is not the same: less pure and more salty, and I'm afraid there is no point in me telling you anything any more.' Oh, well!

But Signora Pasqua, the owner of the Su Gologone hotel, was more forthcoming and told me how her rôtissier made incredibly good *porceddu*. He skewered the piglet from head to tail and left it to drain off its fat for about two hours. After that he rubbed salt on it and put it over the fire. Then he rubbed it all over with a piece of ignited lard. This makes the skin of the pig lacquered in a beautiful brown, the colour of highly polished red mahogany. The *porceddu* is ready in about an hour.

And there they were, four little piglets hanging over the huge fire along one side of the large dining room of the hotel. We started with a little nibbling of pecorino, sausages and *salame* to keep some hunger at bay but preserve our appetite for the *porceddu*. It really was excellent, and I could see why people drive miles and miles to go and have the famous *porceddu* of Su Gologone. When I first went there, some ten years ago, we got totally lost in the mountains of the Barbagia and my husband and I had the usual quarrel all couples have in the car. We arrived at the Su Gologone tired and cross. But it was certainly worth any quarrel. I've never had a piece of pork that tasted so delicious. A tender, sweet and porky lean meat, wrapped in a more porky crust, with a layer of melt-in-the-mouth fat in between. Sheer delight!

BOTTARGA

Bottarga is the dried roe of a female grey mullet or a tuna. The grey mullet *bottarga* is much more delicate and more prized. It is a speciality of Sardinia, while the *bottarga* of tuna is mostly made in Sicily. We went to see Giovanni Spanu of Tradizioni Nostrane in Cabras, near Oristano on the western coast of the island, and for the first time in my life I really ate a *bottarga* that made me realize why some people are passionate about it. It was sweet and delicate and yet full of flavour, without any trace of the metallic aftertaste which *bottarghe* that are not as good have always left in my mouth. It really was a treat, and it will be an even greater treat when I start the one I treasure in the fridge, a gift from Giovanni. I shall slice it fine and pour over it a few drops of my Ligurian olive oil, and then eat it in silence and reverence.

The *bottarga* of Oristano has the reputation of being the best on the island. This is due to the nearby ponds along the coast where the grey mullet come to get warm and eat the flora at the bottom. The fish go into the ponds in May. The water, although sea water, is much warmer than the sea itself and by the end of their stay the mullet become quite big, up to 4 kilos. They get fat and their roe gets full. The fish are caught from the end of September through October, for about forty days, when the roe is at its best.

To make a good *bottarga* the roe must be full but not too full, otherwise it becomes too oily and impossible to dry. The roe is taken out of the fish in its sac and then salted, pressed and dried for about five or six months, by which time it has acquired a beautiful deep amber colour. Salting is a very important process in the success of a good *bottarga*, as is drying. At Giovanni's firm they try to simulate the method of drying in the open air, as it was done in the past, by blowing a gentle breeze of warm air into the large drying rooms.

The drying can take up to a month. This is the artisanal way. When it is *au point*, the *bottarga* is stored in freezers to last until the next lot goes in, or much longer. Giovanni ate some five-year-old *bottarga* and said it was delicious. Well wrapped, in the fridge, it can last a long time.

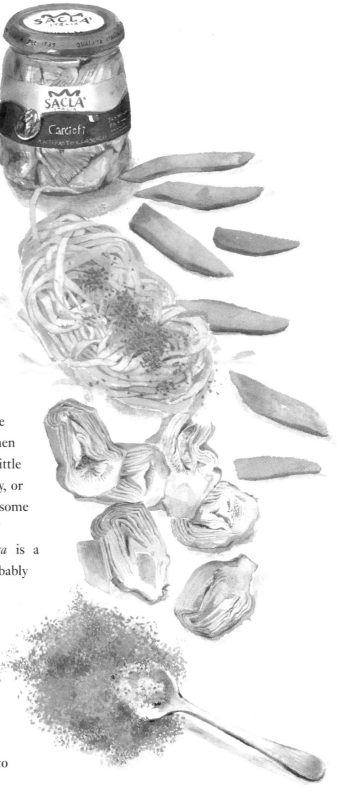

Some *bottarga*, when dried, is grated and put in tins. This grated product is ideal for dressing pasta. After the pasta is cooked, it is stir-fried in oil and garlic and parsley (if you wish) and then, at the very end, some grated *bottarga* – not too much – is sprinkled over it. I asked Giovanni how he liked his *bottarga* best. 'Sliced very thin and just with oil, a good sweet olive oil,' he answered. 'But sometimes, when I'm in the mood, I like to make it a little more substantial and I add a little celery, or some cherry tomatoes or, best of all, some Sardinian artichokes, very thinly sliced.'

Giovanni told us that *bottarga* is a product with a very long history, probably made by the Phoenicians, great seafarers, who used to make another Sardinian speciality, nowadays quite rare: *merca*. The grey mullet, boiled in sea water, is pressed and then wrapped in *salicornia*, an alga found in the sea-salt ponds of Oristano. I have never tasted *merca*, and, in the hope of doing so, I have to keep on going to that fascinating island.

Artichoke Salad

Clean the artichokes – you use only the heart for this recipe. Cut the artichokes in half and then into fine slices lengthwise. Lay them on a plate and sprinkle them with a very little lemon juice (no more then a coffee spoon). Pour over some fruity extra virgin olive oil and sprinkle with salt and pepper. Cut some *bottarga* in thin slices (like you would do with a salami) and add to the artichokes. Mix well and serve.

As a substitute for the artichokes, when they are not in season, you can make a salad of *bottarga* with white celery (finely cut) and cherry tomatoes, halved. Giovanni Spanu, of Tradizioni Nostrane, who gave me this recipe, says that this is really only a substitute, in fact artichokes are deep in Sardinian culture and they plant them even in the flower beds...

If you can't get fresh artichokes you can make the salad with artichokes preserved in oil if they are really good-quality ones.

LE PIANTE E LE ERBE SELVATICHE
WILD PLANTS, WILD HERBS

'*Ma Signora*, here in Sardegna we didn't eat vegetables. We ate wild plants, all those we could gather in the countryside.' So Signora Pasqua Salis Polimodde of the Su Gologone hotel told me. Signora Pasqua owns and runs this lovely hotel, an oasis of beauty, relaxation and excellent food, in the middle of the wild and forbidding Barbagia. This beautiful lady knows the cooking of her beloved island and she certainly reproduces it in the hotel.

The list of edible wild plants is long, and these are just some of the ones that appear frequently in Sardinian cooking. Most of them are used in the filling for ravioli or in savoury pies and tarts, with the ideal accompaniment, pecorino cheese.

First and foremost is myrtle, an evergreen bush with reddish branches, shiny emerald leaves and purple berries. Myrtle is used to flavour roast piglet and other meat and to make liqueurs – white *mirto* from the leaves and red *mirto* from the berries. As with most wild plants, its reputed therapeutic properties are numerous. It is said to help with bronchitis, digestive troubles, diarrhoea and haemorrhoids.

Another popular plant is wild fennel, which is eaten raw in salads, or cooked, sautéd in pure lard. The seeds are used for flavouring biscuits, bread and liqueurs. *Finocchietto* is helpful in fighting nausea, hiccups and rheumatism. Beetroot, another favourite, make the best *frittata* – Italian omelette. They are rich in Vitamin A and in iron; they are laxative, they clarify the complexion, and they stop headaches and other minor illnesses. Watercress, chicory, nasturtium and sorrel are usually eaten raw, dressed only with oil and salt. The thin wild asparagus, found in the spring among stones and thorny bushes, is fried in lard and then mixed with eggs for the most delicious scrambled eggs, or boiled and then covered with slices of cheese. It is good for the heart but bad for the kidneys.

The *corbezzolo* or strawberry tree is a native plant that is often grown in gardens, being the symbol of hospitality. The red berries, which ripen in the autumn, are used to make a jam which has a delicious bitter aftertaste and to make a liqueur. But the best gift the *corbezzolo* gives are the flowers, on which bees feed to make the most divine honey. The *corbezzolo* is good for the liver, the intestines, asthma and the prostate.

But it is the prickly pear that is the iconic plant of Sardinia. Introduced by the Spanish (in Sardinian dialect it is called the Moorish fig), it now dominates the countryside with its massive clumps of elephant-ear branches. While I can admire its architectural shapes, I cannot share the locals' love for the fruit itself. When you eat it, your mouth becomes full of a mush tasting only of sugar. Try it next time you go there, but have it prepared for you by a Sardinian. Once, during a walk when I couldn't resist my passion for 'food for free', I picked one, peeled it and popped it into my curious mouth. For two days I had to put up with the tingling of tiny thorns on my tongue.

Seriola Dumerili

Grilled Ricciola with Chive Sauce

Common English language names for this fish include amberjack, amberfish, yellowtail, Jenny Lind, rock salmon and sailor's choice. Good alternatives to use in this recipe would be firm-fleshed fish such as mahi mahi, sea bass or swordfish.

The best way to enjoy this fish with a firm, white flesh and delicate flavour is to grill it or barbecue it, turning the fish several times during the cooking. The fish is done when golden outside but still pink and moist inside (about 4–5 minutes each side). Serve with the chive sauce below, or the parsley sauce (page 222) and accompany with grilled vegetables.

This recipe comes from Giuseppe Ercole who likes to serve fresh *ricciola* (as well as the *orata*) raw, cutting the fillets into thin slices or chopping them in a tartare, and accompany it with the parsley or the more delicate chive sauce. The sauce is not to marinate the fish but simply an accompaniment.

SERVES 4

FOR THE CHIVE SAUCE

3–4 tablespoons extra virgin olive oil
pinch of salt
½ teaspoon pink peppercorns, crushed

25g/1oz chopped chives
1 hard-boiled egg, chopped

Mix all the ingredients together and serve.

LA SAGRA DELL' UVA IN QUARTU SANT'ELENA

The Grape Festival of Quartu

Quartu Sant'Elena, to the east of Cagliari, is surely one of the least attractive towns in Italy. But that day in September 2006 it seemed to be even beautiful, thanks to the grape Sagra and Saint Elena's Feast.

Saint Elena, born circa 225 AD, was the mother of Constantine, the first Christian Roman Emperor. She went to Jerusalem to find Christ's Cross, and died there. The Sardinians of Quartu decided to make her their patron saint, and on the second weekend in September they throw a *festa*. All the people of Quartu and the neighbouring villages gather in the cathedral and in the square outside to pay homage to the saint, whose statue is carried at the end of the procession on a cart pulled by two magnificent oxen. Huge brown tender-eyed beasts with long horns, dressed with red and white shiny ribbons and red and white scalloped doily caps poised ridiculously between them, they seem conscious of their important role on that day.

The procession opens with the children, all in local costume, followed by the women, who also wear local costume and are covered with jewellery, ranging from exquisite filigree pendants and earrings of Sardinian workmanship to necklaces and chains of Spanish design, which the Sardinians have absorbed during the long Spanish occupation. Both the costumes and the jewellery are handed down from mother to daughter through generations. Val and I talked to a beautiful young girl, so proud to be included at last in the procession, no longer as a child but with the women. She was wearing a magnificent costume handed down to her by her grandmother: her pleated skirt in glowing red and gold was half covered by a black and gold apron; the blouse was white with a starched ruffled collar and cuffs peeking out of a black velvet bolero. But it was her antique jewellery she was particularly proud of: her beautiful golden necklace, an exquisite chain with a filigree pendant, and her earrings.

On one side of the square five black horses were impatiently kicking the air and the road. Two of them were dressed with handsome caparisons in glorious bright colours. We followed the procession down the main road and turned into a courtyard. At the end of it was a long

chapel-like hall, beautifully decorated with vine branches bearing luscious bunches of black and white grapes. Girls dressed in gold and red skirts were handing round little plates of fresh and dried Zibibbo grapes and local *dolci*. I couldn't resist the semi-dried Zibibbo and popped a few half-shrivelled grapes into my mouth. Their aromatic sweetness brought me instantly back to my childhood Christmases in Milan, where little bunches of semi-dried Zibibbo were always on the table among large walnuts and almonds, fat dried figs and dates and bright cheerful mandarins.

Outside in the courtyard there were a few stalls selling local products. I bought my usual *salame*, a *salame al mirto* (myrtle), and it was one of the very best salami I brought back from Italy. Val and I were transfixed by the handiwork of Assunta, a woman at one of the *dolci* stalls. She was making tiny almond paste roses in pink and green with tremendous speed and utter precision. She asked me to pop one in my mouth but I was reluctant to swallow such a painstaking work of art. She insisted and I gave in, and my mouth was filled with the most delicate orangey-almond scent.

We ended the evening in Cagliari, with a superb dinner in a most luxurious restaurant, S'Apposentu. The contrast between our two experiences was incredible. From a feast which gave us a glimpse and a taste of old Sardinia, we were catapulted into a sleek contemporary restaurant situated in the very modern opera house of Cagliari, all grey stone and white wood. We had the *menu gastronomico*, of some ten courses, of which the triumphs were *gnocchetti sardi* with aubergine and shrimp (see page 237) and thin slices of smoked swordfish containing a divine onion ice-cream. Sardinia is indeed an unpredictable, mysterious land.

LA PASTA SARDA

SARDINIAN PASTA

Malloreddus

Also known as *gnocchetti sardi* when made industrially. The name *malloreddus* usually refers to the pasta made at home with durum wheat, semolina and water. It is made by pressing a small lump of the dough, the size of a finger-nail, over a basket in such a way that it makes the little lump turn over and become grooved. Originally *malloreddus* were dressed only with pecorino, but when tomatoes arrived in Italy, tomato sauce became the more common dressing. Other popular dressings are sausages or wild boar *ragù*.

Alisansas

Large, short strips of pasta, 2cm x 5cm, made with brown flour, very hot water and 2 or 3 eggs for each kilogram of flour. Signora Pasqua of the Su Gologone hotel stressed to me that the water must be very hot and the pasta must be made on a wooden board and, of course, with a wooden rolling pin. The dough is kneaded for a long time but it is not stretched thin – about 3mm. *Alisansas* should be cut with a pastry wheel. Once dried they are boiled in the usual way and dressed with a *ragù* of aubergine, or with fungi or chicken giblets.

Maccarones de busa

The name means *maccheroni* with a hole. They are made by hand with durum wheat semolina and water. They are made by rolling two small balls of dough over a knitting needle. They can be dressed in most ways, from simple pecorino and ricotta to a lavish *ragù* of lamb and pork or of game.

Sa fregola

This is the Sardinian couscous, made with coarsely ground durum wheat semolina and salted water. It is made in a basin, adding the water slowly with a circling movement of the hand. It is a very difficult pasta to make, and these days is mostly made by elderly women. There is an old song in which the girl in love pleads to her beloved, 'Marry me, I can make fregola.' Fregola is cooked in stock with fresh cheese or added to vegetable soups.

Su filindeu

This is made with semolina, flour, water and salt. The dough is kneaded very hard for a long time until it forms threads (*fili*). Signora Pasqua, who was unravelling the mysteries of Sardinian pasta-making for me, asked one of her girls to bring me a piece of *filindeu*. And there in front of me the girl put a square piece of pasta made from thin threads stuck together. 'Like a piece of cloth,' said Signora Pasqua. That 'piece of cloth' is cooked in stock, usually goat stock. This is a traditional pasta of the Barbagia, to which I found no references in other parts of the island.

Culurgiones

Also called *angiolottus*, these are large ravioli filled with very fresh pecorino (it should still be dripping whey), aged pecorino, spinach and eggs. In the old days *culurgiones* were filled only with ricotta and pecorino. They are usually dressed with the plainest tomato sauce.

Malloreddus

Malloreddus with Prawn Sauce and Aubergine

Malloreddus are small Sardinian *gnocchi*. This Sardinian pasta was perfect dressed with this sauce, a version of a traditional recipe created by the chef of the Ristorante S'Apposentu in Cagliari, which we enjoyed in October 2006.

SERVES 4

275g/10oz semolina flour
extra virgin olive oil
a handful of finely chopped spring onions
1 garlic clove, chopped
1 aubergine, chopped

150g/5oz red crawfish, shelled
a handful of fresh parsley, chopped
saffron, preferably from San Gavino Monreale
cooking water from 10 mussels, or a fish stock cube
a handful of wild thyme leaves

To make the dough for the *malloreddus*, put the flour into a large bowl and add enough water to make a soft dough. Cover tightly with cling film and leave to rest in a cool place for 1 hour.

Heat 3 tablespoons of olive oil in a saucepan and add the spring onions and half the garlic. Cook over a moderate heat for a minute, then add the aubergine and continue to cook until soft. Remove the mixture from the pan and set aside.

Heat a little more oil in the same pan and cook the crawfish with the remaining garlic and the parsley for a few minutes. As soon as the crawfish change colour, remove the pan from the heat and add the mussel cooking water or fish stock. Remove the crawfish heads and put the bodies back into the pan. Squeeze out the juices from the heads into the pan and discard the heads. Add the cooked aubergine mixture and the saffron to the pan and leave the sauce to rest.

Unwrap your dough and break off pieces the size of a chickpea. Press each piece of dough against the tines of a fork and then, with your finger, gently roll the pressed dough back off the fork. This takes a little practice. If you find the dough sticking to the fork, dip the fork in flour before you press the dough against it.

To cook the *malloreddus*, drop them into a pot of boiling water. After a few minutes they will float to the top, which means they are ready. Remove them with a slotted spoon and add them to the crawfish sauce with a little of their cooking water. Cook for a few minutes on a high heat, stirring until the sauce has thickened. Remove from the heat, season with salt and pepper, and add the thyme and 2 or 3 tablespoons of olive oil. Serve hot.

IL PANE
BREAD

In Sardinia bread-making used to be a rite. The mistress of the house, after crossing herself, would begin to bring together the flour or semolina in a large basin with salt and water. Then she would add the yeast and divide the large mass into as many balls as there were women around the table to help. The balls, kneaded first, would be left to rise, then kneaded again and shaped, then left again, covered with a cloth, while the women had a coffee and a chat. They needed a rest because 'bread to be good needs shoulder oil' as the Sardinian saying goes. After that the loaves would be baked and for a month there would be bread, ready to go on the table. Oddly enough, it is only in Sardinia that the women are the bread-makers, and for the village feasts, for weddings, christenings and funerals they express this craft to the full.

The Sardinian bread par excellence is *pane carasau*, also called *carta da musica*, a type of bread made only on the island. A disc of dough, about 30cm across, is baked, and when cooked it is cut in half horizontally to make two very thin and friable discs which are baked again for a short time. This bread can be kept for months, and indeed it used to be the bread shepherds took with them during their long journeys, to eat with pecorino cheese.

Many other shapes of bread are made. The crumb or the crust might be different, as well as the shape – large and round, with a hole like a ring, long like a baguette, shaped like a crown, a plait or a bun – or whatever took the fancy of the bread-maker. The biggest *pagnotta* can weigh 5kg and more.

When we were in Barbagia we went to see an extraordinary museum in the town of Oliena. The museum was in the house of the town doctor, who, when he died, left the house to the town. The house consists of a number of rooms and courtyards, all higgledy-piggledy, one after the other or around the other. In that fascinating setting the locals have set up the Bread Museum. In the first room there are all the different flours and semolina, sieves, tools and cloths used to make bread, while in the last room all the festive and ceremonial breads are on show. Some of the wedding breads are like elaborate sculptures or antique jewels, while for children's celebrations there are little horses, dolls, birds, boats, pretty bags and other toys. For Easter the breads, shaped as baskets or birds, lambs or doves, contain eggs. For Palm Sunday breads are made in the shape of palm fronds, olive branches or crosses, and for funerals there are wreaths of beautifully shaped leaves speckled with berries.

I found it quite awesome that in a lost town, in the middle of the wildest part of Sardinia, a museum had been established to commemorate *il pane*. It is the most tangible proof of the importance of this food in the culture and life of the island.

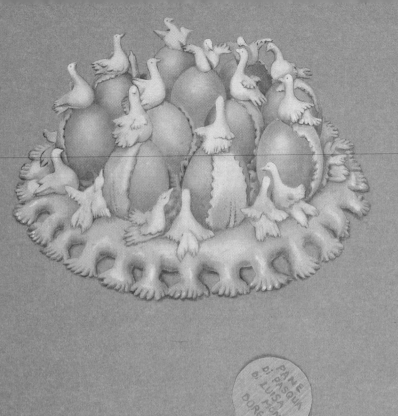

PANE
DI PASQUA
DI LUISA
MONNE
D'ORGALI

corona della
sposa
OLIENA

PECORINO AND FIORE SARDO

With over 3 million sheep on their island it is no wonder that the Sardinians are the world-wide experts in making ewe cheeses. You wander off the *superstrada* that cuts the island across vertically, you stop and launch out into the countryside for a walk among the Mediterranean *maquis* and you are accompanied everywhere by the distant ding-dong of bells. Only in Sardinia do the sheep have bells with such a musical sound. The animals are big and the flocks are huge, guarded by two or three sheepdogs. When they move from one pasture to another, or back to base to be milked, the shepherd goes with them – quite often, nowadays – in a car. Alas, it seems that the bucolic sight of the shepherd, crook in hand, following his flock, is lost for ever.

The centre of Sardinia, forbidding and wild, is where the best cheeses are made, thanks to all the different scented herbs eaten by the sheep. Last September Val and I went to visit the Azienda Agricola of Pinuccio Podda in Orolai, near Orgosolo. Pinuccio and his brother Giovanni welcomed us in their caseificio or cheese dairy, set in a most beautiful valley surrounded by woods of ilexes and pines. Unfortunately it was no longer the cheese-making season. Ewe cheeses are made from about January to June, and the milk is at its best in the spring.

OPPOSITE: *Easter and wedding breads*

The milk the Podda brothers use comes entirely from their own sheep, which are raised on semi-wild pastures. The cheeses are made in the same way that the Poddas' father and grandfathers and great-grandfathers have made them all through the centuries. From some low buildings across the yard, a symphony of grunts and squeaks was emanating. 'Those are the pigs,' said Giovanni, and he went into one of the pig-sties and came back with a beautiful fat pink piglet. 'They are fed on the waste from the cheeses, the best food for them.'

After the caseificio we went to the shop. You enter a courtyard through an archway – *il cortile del formaggio* – and you are surrounded at once by a subtle cheesy aroma. A cheesy smell can be rather unpleasant, but in that courtyard full of pots of flowers and herbs it was extremely pleasing, mixed with the scent of the sage and rosemary. In the spotlessly clean shop, more like a cave in the rock, Pinuccio's sister Amata was cutting chunks of *fiore sardo* and pecorino for us.

There was young pecorino, of about two months, and pecorino aged for about four months. And then there was *fiore sardo*, with its strong flavour and deep smell. This is the oldest cheese made on the island, apparently preceding the Roman conquest of the third century BC. The cheese is produced only with ewe's milk, salt and lamb's rennet. It is dried in caves where a fire burns on the ground, so that the cheese acquires a very slightly smoked flavour. The fresh *fiore sardo*, a table cheese, is aged for three and a half months, while the grating cheese is aged for a minimum of six months. The ricotta made in Sardinia from the whey of the ewe's milk, called *ricotta mustia*, is absolutely delicious. As a table cheese it is slightly salted, smoked and aged for a short time, but it is aged for longer when used grated on pasta.

We left the *cortile del formaggio* loaded with cheeses and walked around Orgosolo to look at the murals, for which the town is famous. Murals have been painted everywhere, some good, some less good and some bad, but all of a political inspiration, mostly inspired by Picasso's *Guernica*. The first mural was painted in 1979 by a Sienese painter married to a local girl. Now, Giovanni told us, painters come from everywhere, even abroad, to adorn his beloved town. And people flock to Orgosolo to see them, as we noticed while following a queue of German tourists.

Val and I decided we much preferred the cheeses.

Sebadas

In Sardinia these are served with bitter corbezzolo honey.

SERVES 4

FOR THE PASTRY
500g/1lb 2oz flour
3 tablespoons lard
a pinch of salt

250g/9oz fresh **pecorino** *cheese*
oil, for frying
corbezzolo honey, sweet honey or sugar
grated zest of 1 unwaxed lemon (optional)

Put the flour, lard and salt into a bowl and add enough warm water to make a dough. Roll out lightly on a floured board with a rolling pin and cut out circles the size of a cup. Place a ball of cheese on each circle, cover with another sheet of pastry and seal the edges using a large glass or a knife.

Fry the cheese pastries in plenty of oil until they are golden, then remove from the heat and drain on kitchen paper. Serve immediately, with honey or sugar. If you like, you can sprinkle them with grated lemon zest.

Pane Frattau

Frattau means grated, and it refers to the grated pecorino cheese that is the crucial ingredient of this simple peasant dish. The other essential ingredient is *pane carasau*, the versatile unleavened Sardinian flatbread.

SERVES 4

4 ripe tomatoes, peeled and deseeded
salt
4 slices of **pane carasau** *(flatbread)*

4 eggs
200g/7oz aged pecorino, grated

Put the tomatoes into a small pan. Simmer for 10 minutes, adding a small amount of hot water and a pinch of salt.

Meanwhile, fill a large pan three-quarters full of water and put on to the heat. When the water reaches roughly 70°C/150°F, i.e. hot but not yet boiling, dip in the *carasau* bread just for a few seconds, once slice at the time. Remove the slices with a ladle and carefully transfer each bread sheet on to an individual serving plate. Pour some of the warm tomato sauce over each bread sheet and spread it out.

Bring a medium-sized pan of water to the boil. Break an egg into the water and carefully, using a small spoon, fold the white over the egg yolk. Simmer for 3 minutes. Using a slotted spoon, transfer the *uovo in camicia* (poached egg) on top of one of the tomato *carasau*. Repeat the same procedure with the other 3 eggs. Sprinkle with plenty of pecorino and serve.

OPPOSITE: *Aged pecorino and pane carasau*

FIORE SARDO DOP

THE ARTICHOKE

'The Artichoke has the virtue of provoking Venus in both Men and Women and for Women of making them more desirable and helping Men who are in these matters rather tardy.' So wrote Bartolomeo Boldo, a doctor of medicine, in 1576. Its supposed aphrodisiac qualities apart, the artichoke is a very versatile vegetable, being excellent boiled, stewed, stuffed, fried in batter, made into a risotto or a *sformato*, transformed into a pasta sauce, or, simply, sliced very thin and eaten raw, dressed with a delicate olive oil and a sprinkling of salt.

The origins of the artichoke are recorded in legend. Zeus fell in love with a beautiful maiden on the Aegean island of Zinari. She dared to disobey him and he turned her into an edible thistle, which was named *Cynara*. This thistle was already greatly appreciated by the Greeks and the Romans. Apicius, the first-century cookery writer, has three recipes for artichokes, all simple. The artichoke, raw or boiled, is dressed with olive oil and herbs, or a cumin dressing. One recipe is very similar to a modern one in that the sauce also contains chopped hard-boiled eggs.

Artichokes are mentioned in the first cookery manuscripts of the fifteenth century, although at the time they were viewed with a certain suspicion. The fifteenth-century poet Ludovico Ariosto wrote that 'you find in them hardness, thorns and bitterness more than goodness'. But by the sixteenth century artichokes were extremely popular in Italy. Although Caterina de' Medici has been wrongly credited with bringing many gastronomic novelties to France, she did introduce the artichoke to the French court when she went there to marry the Dauphin in 1533. She was extremely partial to them and, as a matter of fact, to a lot of other food. The story goes that at the wedding of an aristocratic lady she became ill by eating far too many artichoke hearts and cock's-combs. A woman of great taste, it seems to me, since I share those passions. Alas, cock's-combs are things of the past, but artichoke hearts are one of the joys one can still have in Italy, a joy that makes an Italian winter far more pleasurable. Italy is the biggest producer of artichokes. They grow in all regions where the winters are not too severe, and they are on the market from late October to May. There are many varieties: some with thorns, like the fat Spinoso Violetto di Palermo, the slimmer Spinoso di Liguria and the small artichokes known as *castraure* from the Venetian *laguna*, some thornless, like the round purple Romanesco, the even more purple Violetto di Foggia and the green Precoce di Chioggia.

When we were in Sardinia, Val and I went to visit the large *carciofaia*, or artichoke plantation, of the Sanna family. Francesco Sanna, a charming and enthusiastic third-generation *carciofi* grower, showed us round the fields and explained the long preparation of the soil, the care in the actual growing of the noble thistle and the harvesting, a gruelling job that must be, and can only be, done by hand. Each plant yields about ten *capolini* – heads. Sanna grows two types of artichoke, the Spinoso di Sardegna and the Violetto di Foggia. The latter are perfect for preserving. They are prepared on the spot, cut into halves or quarters depending on their size and put into an acidulated liquid. Some are then sent to the Sacla' workshop in Asti, where they are placed in jars, seasoned with a little salt, garlic and herbs and covered with olive oil. They are very good, with very little vinegary flavour and just the right amount of herbs and garlic to enhance, and not kill, their delicate flavour.

The Spinoso di Sardegna, like all the other varieties with thorns, are best eaten raw as we had them at the local restaurant, *foglia per foglia* – bract by bract – dipping each *foglia* in a pale green pool of Sardinian oil and scraping the soft part away with our teeth, until we reached the heavenly heart. This we cut up in thin slices (no choke here) and used them to mop up the last of the oil, finally popping them into our mouths with a morsel of the Sardinian flatbread, *pane carasau*.

Artichokes in the Pot

This is a simple, classic recipe based on the one given to me by Signora Pasqua of the Su Gologone hotel. You must make it with small, young, thornless artichokes.

Prepare the artichokes as usual, removing all the outside leaves and the choke from the centre. Put them into a basin of acidulated water. Cut off the stalks, peel and cut into segments.

Take an earthenware pot that you can put directly on the heat. Place the artichokes in it, stalk end down. Place the stalk segments here and there among the artichokes. Add enough water to come about halfway up the artichokes and about 8 tablespoons of olive oil. Chop 3 tablespoons parsley, 1–2 garlic cloves and 5–10 mint leaves together, add salt and pepper and add to the pot. Cover with a lid and cook until tender when pierced – about 35–40 minutes. If there is too much liquid, reduce quickly. Serve the artichokes warm or at room temperature with the reduced stock poured over just before serving.

I DOLCI
SWEETS

When I started looking into this subject I found that there are more sweets – biscuits, cakes, sweet breads, all such things – in Sardinia than in any other region of Italy. This is certainly due to the fact that all sorts of old traditions are still very much alive on the island. Epiphany arrives and on the table appears the right *dolce*, followed by the same for Sant'Antonio (17 January), for Carnival, for San Giuseppe, Easter, Ascension Day, and so on, all year round until Christmas.

I am listing here just a fraction of the *dolci* I ate or saw in Sardinia. These are the more common ones.

Pabasinas

These are the traditional biscuits of Easter, All Saints' Day and Christmas. They are made with flour, sugar, almonds and sultanas (*pabassa* in Sardinian dialect). After baking they are iced and covered with multi-coloured sugar balls.

Zippulas

These are the carnival fritters, traditionally shaped like long sausages and covered generously with icing sugar.

Pardulas

Made for Easter with bread dough, *pardulas* are shaped like small baskets and filled with fresh cheese or ricotta flavoured with saffron. After they have been baked, they are spread with honey.

Suspirus

These are possibly the best-known Sardinian biscuits. They are made with ground almonds and sugar and, once baked, they are covered with an icing flavoured with lemon. The lovely name of these biscuits means 'sighs'.

Sebadas or seadas

Large ravioli filled with fresh pecorino cheese. They are fried and covered with honey, sugar and sometimes grated lemon zest. This is my favourite Sardinian pud. (see recipe on page 243.

Pistiddus

Also called *ziricas*, these are sweet pastry tartlets containing a paste made with *sapa* – concentrated wine must – and sugar and flavoured with coffee.

Cocciuleddas de meli

These pretty biscuits, shaped like a snail, are a speciality of Gallura in northern Sardinia. A thin outer shell of pastry is wrapped round a soft filling of ground walnuts and almonds, candied orange rind, cinnamon, cocoa and honey.

Pirichitus

These are the popular *dolci* of Cagliari. They consist of light balls of choux pastry, the size of golf balls, fried and flavoured with orange flour and coated with lemon-flavoured icing.

Pompias

Pompias take their name from the fruit from which they are made. *Pompia* is a spontaneous citrus tree that grows only in Sardinia. The fruit is very large, of a bright yellow colour similar to a citron, and with the flavour of Seville orange and grapefruit mixed together. Only the rind is eaten. The rind, either cut into rounds or left whole in its original shape, is boiled and then immersed in honey. When it is boiled whole, the *pompia* is sometimes filled with chopped almond and is called *pompia prena* – full.

Aranzadas

These *dolci* are small rectangular shaped sweets made up of chopped orange rind, chopped almond and honey, similar to a soft nougat. They are a particular speciality of Nuoro and its province.

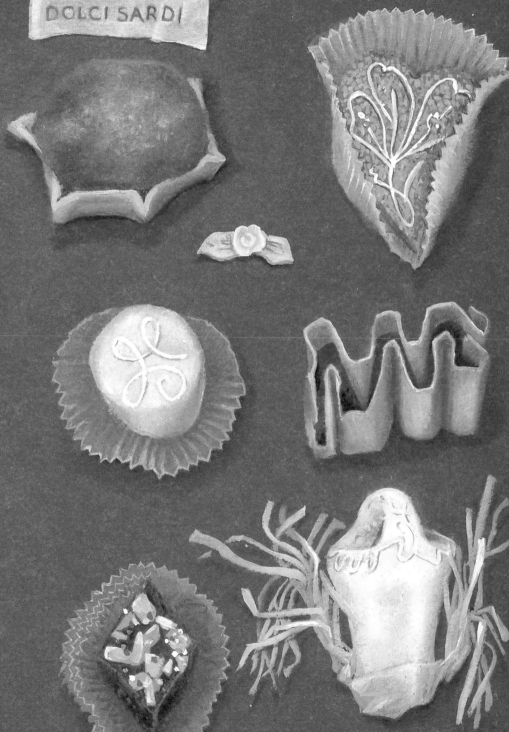

Index

Acknowledgements

Thanks go to Carlo, Lorenzo and Giuseppe Ercole. The original idea for this book came from Clare Blampied, Managing Director of Sacla' in the UK, and Roger Jupe, a food marketing consultant. Their vision was to bring food and painting, the two arts that feed the body and soul of the Italian way of life, together in one evocative book.

RECIPE ACKNOWLEDGEMENTS

33 'Risotto al Gorgonzola'; 109 'Coniglio con Olive e Pinoli'; 132 'Torta Pasqualina'; 147 'Piccioni a Letto'; 198 'Purè di Fave con Cicorie, Cipolle e Olive' and 244 'Pane Frattau' adapted from *Ricette di Osterie d'Italia*. Reprinted by permission of Slow Food Editore.

62 'Gnocchi di Patate con Zucchero e Cannella'; 66 'Faraona in Peverada' and 75 'Sarde in Saor' adapted from *Ricette di Osterie del Veneto*. Reprinted by permission of Slow Food Editore.

74 'Risotto Nero'; 76 'Baccalà alla Vicentina' and 83 'Bigoli in Salsa all' Ebraica' adapted from *Cucina Veneziana* by Giuseppe Maffioli, published by Franco Muzzio Editore.

89 'Rice and Peas' and 101 'Galani' reproduced from *The Da Fiore Cookbook* by Damiano Martin Copyright © Damiano Martin 2004. Reprinted by permission of HarperCollins Publishers.

129 'Stuffed Zucchini' from *Recipes from Paradise* by Fred Plotkin. Reprinted with permission.

188 'Involtini di Carne e Melanzane' and 211 'Tria e Cicieri' adapted from *Odori, Sapori, Colori della Cucina Salentina* by Lazari Lucia. Reprinted by permission of Congedo Editore.

210 'Orecchiette alle Cime di Rapa e Peperoncino' reproduced from *Made In Italy* by Giorgio Locatelli. Copyright © Giorgio Locatelli 2007. Reprinted by permission of HarperCollins Publishers Ltd.

Every effort has been made to contact the copyright holders. We apologise in advance for any unintentional omissions and would be pleased to insert the appropriate acknowledgement in any subsequent publication.

AUTHOR'S ACKNOWLEDGEMENTS

First and foremost I want to thank Clare Blampied for asking me to write this book. I enjoyed writing it and I enjoyed even more visiting all the places with Val, the painter, and Roger Jupe. Thank you Roger for being the most reliable and confident driver and an excellent navigator. My thanks also go to Lucia Ercole and Sara Sacco Botto for organizing all the travel plans and schedules and for arranging so efficiently the many interviews we undertook. All these people have been mentioned in the texts of different regions. Here, I'd like to thank them all for the time they spared and for the invaluable information they provided.